Pruning
&
Pest Control

Graham
Rice
&
Alan
Titchmarsh

TREASURE PRESS

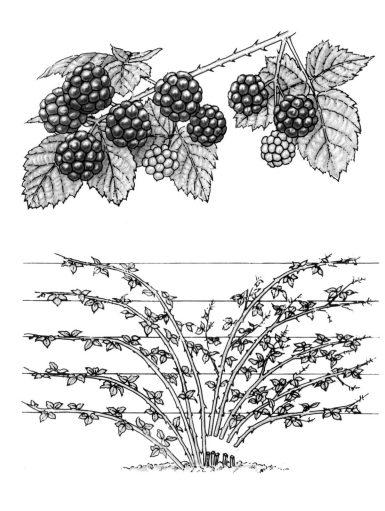

Material contained in this book was
previously published in *Pruning* and
Pest Free Plants

First published in Great Britain in 1983 by
Octopus Books Limited

This edition published in 1987 by
Treasure Press
59 Grosvenor Street
London W1

© 1983 Octopus Books Limited

ISBN 1 85051 175 6

Printed in Hong Kong

Contents

Illustrations by

Josephine Martin 2, 30-33
Russell Barnet 4-7, 16-19, 28, 29, 36, 37, 39
Gary Marsh 9-15
Garden Studio: Bob Bampton 22-27, 41-43
    Liz Pepperal 44, 45
Jillian Burgess: David Salariya 47, 50
    Ed Roberts 52-67
    Nicholas Hall 70-85
    David Wright 89-93, 95

GUIDE TO GOOD PRUNING

WHY PRUNE?
- To improve the shape of the plant
- To restrict the plant to a particular size
- To produce an abundance of attractive foliage stems
- To promote better flowering
- To encourage larger and better fruits

SHAPE Most shrubs look best when their natural shape is retained. In most situations the 'buns' and 'boxes' produced by over-zealous clipping should be avoided, unless, of course, you intend to practise topiary.

SIZE If summer flowering shrubs are cut annually to about 7.5 cm (3 in) they will never grow larger than the length of one year's growth. The same shrub could be cut back each year to a taller framework to allow for underplanting. Removing less or none of the growth made the previous year will lead to tall, ungainly specimens, with flowers at the top of spindly stems. Hard pruning usually results in a small number of vigorous shoots, while light pruning produces more less-vigorous shoots.

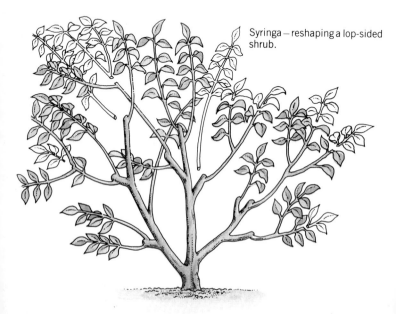

Syringa – reshaping a lop-sided shrub.

FOLIAGE AND STEMS

Plants with variegated or coloured leaves can be pruned to emphasise these features, although at the expense of flowers or fruit. The Purple Smoke Bush, *Cotinus coggygria* 'Royal Purple', and the variegated Weigela, *Weigela florida* 'Variegata', are good examples. For the best foliage, these should be cut back to three or four buds once they start to grow in the spring. Evergreens should be treated less severely than deciduous subjects and should be pruned a little later.

With the variegated and yellow leaved varieties there may be a tendency to reversion – that is, the occasional green shoot may appear amongst the coloured ones. Reverted shoots are usually far more vigorous and should be cut right out at their point of origin, or gradually they will swamp the rest of the plant.

Some Dogwoods (Cornus) and Willows (Salix) are grown for their brightly coloured stems, which are a valuable contribution to the garden in the winter. The colour of the young growth is the most effective, so these shrubs should be cut back hard in early spring.

Cornus alba – cut back hard in spring to encourage colourful new growth.

FLOWERS

To obtain a good floral display the growth that produces the most flowers must be encouraged. Buddleias, for example, flower on the current season's wood, which means the shoots that have grown earlier the same year. So, in order to promote good flowering, these shoots must be encouraged to make as much strong growth as possible during the season, and are cut back hard in the spring. As a result, the flowers will be twice the size of those on unpruned plants.

Other shrubs, such as Philadelphus, produce their flowers on shoots that have grown the previous year, so if these are cut hard in the spring all the flower buds will be cut off and they will not flower until the following season. These shrubs, therefore, should always be pruned *after* flowering.

Bedding plants also need to be pruned, or rather pinched back. By pinching back the central shoot of Antirrhinums to 10 cm (4 in) the plant will be stimulated into making much more bushy growth, with each side shoot producing a flower spike. For a profusion of flowers other bedding plants should be treated in the same way.

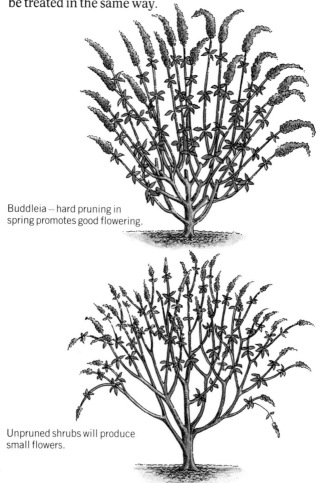

Buddleia — hard pruning in spring promotes good flowering.

Unpruned shrubs will produce small flowers.

FRUIT

Flowers ultimately lead to fruit so the same pruning guidelines apply. The aim must always be to encourage productive growth, though the method will vary with the type of crop. Vines, raspberries, peaches, apples and figs, all fruit in different ways and so need different treatment. Vines, for example, should always be pruned in winter as they may bleed to death if pruned in spring or summer.

Although large crops are the obvious aim, there can come a point when the tree bears too many fruits and their size is inevitably reduced. If the crop is thinned out the individual fruits will be much larger. An apple tree bearing large clusters of fruit irregularly spaced along the branch, will produce smaller apples than if the same number of fruits were spread more evenly along the branch.

If a shrub is grown for its ornamental fruits then the desire to retain these on the plant for as long as possible forces a change in pruning practice. Whereas pruning would normally take place after flowering, when dealing with ornamental trees and shrubs it is necessary to wait until after they have finished fruiting.

Apple
Clusters of large fruit.

Small, poor quality fruit.

TOOLS

Pruning tools should always be kept clean and sharp. Blunt tools are difficult to use and will also damage and bruise the shoots or branches. As with most items of equipment, buy the best tools you can afford. The initial expense will be amply repaid over the years, for good quality tools will last longer, stay sharp for longer and enable you to make cleaner cuts with less effort.

SECATEURS

These are an essential piece of equipment for most gardeners. They vary in size and design but there are two main types: the anvil, with one cutting blade, and the by-pass, with two cutting blades. Before buying a pair of secateurs try them in your hand to make sure that they are comfortable and the right size, and that you can operate them easily without exerting too much pressure. The smaller models are often suitable for taking cuttings as well as light pruning.

Anvil type secateurs have a single sharp blade which cuts the wood on a flat anvil. Always place the blade *above* a bud when making a cut and do keep the blade sharp and the anvil clean. Do not twist the secateurs when cutting. With this type of secateur there can be a tendency to squash the stems, although if the blade is kept sharp this will be minimised.

A fairly recent design has a sliding, rather than a pincer-like action, and can cut thicker wood than other secateurs of the same size.

By-pass type secateurs are probably the most popular. These cut with a scissor action though only the upper blade has a cutting edge. By-pass type secateurs should be used with the slim cutting blade uppermost. One model has a swivelling lower handle which helps to prevent blistered fingers and is therefore particularly useful if you are doing a lot of pruning. The heavier models can cut wood up to about 2 cm (¾ in) thick.

• Never try to cut thicker wood than the secateurs can comfortably manage.

• Always clean off ingrained dirt, and oil the secateurs after use.

• Keep the blades closed and the catch on when the secateurs are not in use.

• Store the secateurs in a safe place out of the reach of children.

Long arm or long handled secateurs are useful for cutting old, hard wood which is too tough or thick for ordinary secateurs to cope with. The long handles provide extra leverage and branches up to 2.5 cm (1 in) in diameter can be cut much more easily. The long handles also give them greater reach. However, do not be tempted to wrestle with them and try and cut thick branches. This not only puts considerable strain on the tools but also makes a ragged cut.

Long loppers are simply large secateurs mounted on a very long handle (up to 3.65 m/12 ft) and operated by a wire. If you don't like ladders and heights they are invaluable for removing high branches which would otherwise be out of reach, although they are only suitable for wood up to about 2.5 cm (1 in) in diameter. A saw attachment will deal with thicker wood, though it's hard work. A fruit-gathering attachment is also available.

HAND SHEARS

These are useful for clipping small hedges, and trimming heathers after flowering to remove the dead heads. Most hand shears have a notch in the jaws for cutting heavier wood, as the blades themselves will only cut light twigs. Don't strain them by trying to cut heavier growth. A large pair of scissors can also be used to trim heathers. There are also various other types of hand clippers available, which, although operated with one hand, cut horizontally.

For very long, or tall hedges, electric clippers are a worthwhile investment, although a cheaper and useful alternative is the hedge trimming attachment for electric drills, which is very quick and efficient.

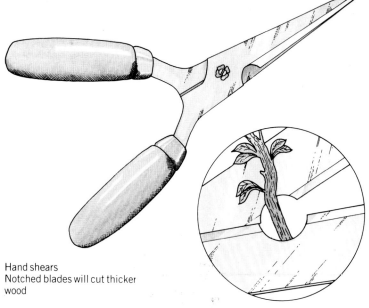

Hand shears
Notched blades will cut thicker wood

SAWS

For cutting wood which is over 2.5 cm (1 in) in diameter a saw is essential. Ordinary carpentry saws should not be used as they are not efficient at cutting green wood, and are often much too large.

Folding saw The narrow blade will cut wood up to 5 cm (2 in) in diameter, but it can be hard work on wood that is much thicker.

Grecian saw The curved blade cuts more quickly and efficiently than a straight-bladed saw.

Double sided saw The coarse teeth on one side are for live wood, and the fine teeth on the other edge for dead, dry wood. Take care not to damage branches with the side not being used for cutting.

Bow saw Sometimes called a log saw. Metal 'bow' with replaceable blades. Comes in several sizes for heavier branches.

Chain saw Electric or petrol versions are available. The greatest care should be taken when using them. This type of saw makes light work of all heavy wood but can be very dangerous if not used responsibly.

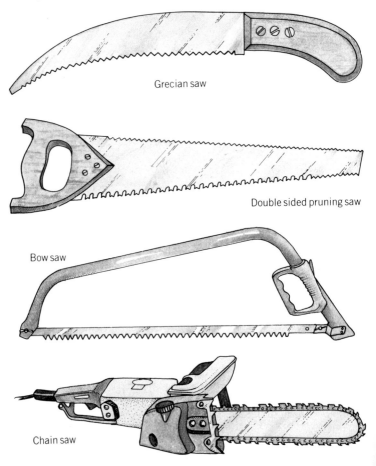

Grecian saw

Double sided pruning saw

Bow saw

Chain saw

SAFETY
Most tools can be dangerous if used wrongly, so always take care and follow the guidelines below:

- Keep all tools clean and well maintained.

- Never put equipment under undue strain, or use it for work for which it was never designed.

- Keep all tools and equipment out of the reach of children.

- Never operate electric tools in wet conditions and always use the right fuse.

- Keep power cables well away from the cutting blades when using electric tools.

- If a knife is used for pruning, keep it sharp – it is much safer to use than a blunt one.

- Never attempt to fell large trees. Leave that type of work for a qualified tree surgeon.

- Never climb into a tree to cut off branches.

- Wear gloves when pruning spiny plants.

- If you accidentally cut or graze yourself, particularly if this occurs on agricultural land, consult your doctor, who may recommend an anti-tetanus injection.

Ladders should always be securely supported.

MISCELLANEOUS TOOLS

Knives should only be used by the experienced gardener and then only with great care. They are, however, valuable for paring the edges of large saw cuts before applying protective paint.

Rope is useful when felling small trees to ensure that they fall in the right direction, and for tying in ladders.

Proprietary wound paints based on bitumen, and usually containing a fungicide, are essential to prevent infection, particularly for larger pruning cuts.

Gloves, although often scorned, are important for protecting your hands against minor cuts and grazes. Tightly stitched leather gloves are particularly useful for pruning thorny shrubs and old roses. Choose ones with long wrists to keep out thorns and other debris.

Ladders should always be well maintained. Keep the rungs free from paint and grease. When using a ladder for pruning, make sure that it is securely tied to the tree, or at least supported by another person.

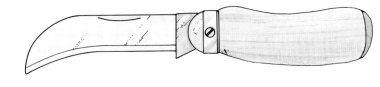

A sharp pruning knife is useful
for paring off the ends of large
saw cuts.

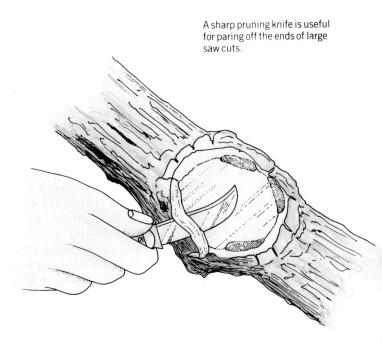

MAINTENANCE
Looking after your tools will make them last longer, and perform much more efficiently.

1. Dirt and grime are the perfect breeding grounds for disease – to prevent the spread of infection all tools should be thoroughly cleaned after use.

2. Use emery paper to clean the grime off secateurs and to hone finely the cutting blades.

3. Protect saw blades by wiping with an oily rag after use.

4. Never leave tools out in the garden.

5. Check cables on electric tools and repair any damaged plastic coating or exposed wires.

6. Store all tools in a safe, dry place well out of reach of children.

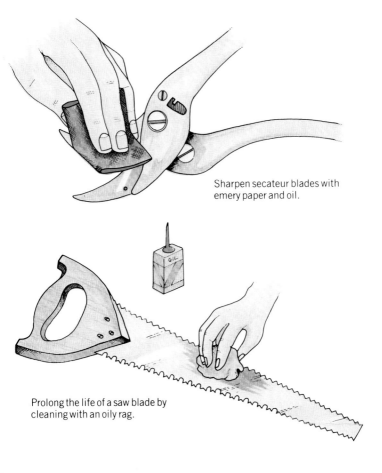

Sharpen secateur blades with emery paper and oil.

Prolong the life of a saw blade by cleaning with an oily rag.

PRUNING TECHNIQUES

HOW TO CUT   There are three essential requirements for a good pruning cut:

> - It should be a clean cut with no ragged edges.
> - It should be just above a bud leaving no snag.
> - It should slope slightly away from the bud so that water runs away from the bud.

Pruning cuts which do not fulfil these requirements are *bad* cuts and will lead to disease.

Too far from bud

Sloping the wrong way

Too close to bud

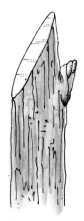

Too sharp an angle

Ragged cut

Correct cut

HOW TO SAW

When removing the branch of a tree the aim should be to cut the limb cleanly and flush with the trunk or larger branch. Saw off the bulk of the branch, making an undercut first to prevent the bark from tearing. A top cut is then made a little further up the branch. The remaining stump is removed with a single cut.

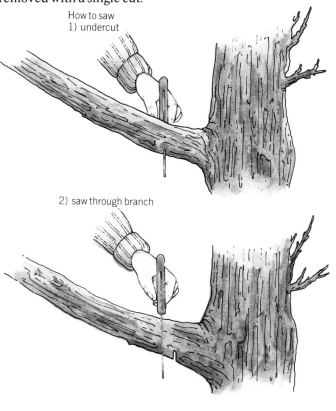

How to saw
1) undercut

2) saw through branch

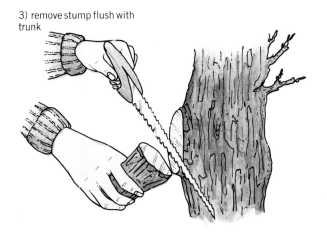

3) remove stump flush with trunk

ROSES

Almost all roses need regular pruning to keep them healthy, encourage flowering and maintain their shape; all except shrub roses need to be pruned every year. The best time for pruning is undoubtedly the spring, when the roses are just starting into growth. This also enables you to put right any damage which may occur during the winter months.

PLANTING Bare-root roses are always planted during the winter when the plants are dormant. They should always be pruned *before* planting, unless, of course, this has already been done by the nurseryman. Trim back long or damaged roots and cut the tops back about 23 cm (9 in), but leave the serious formative pruning until the buds begin to shoot in spring. At this point the degree of pruning must be tailored to the particular type of rose, but most varieties are usually cut back hard during the first year. Container-grown plants, which can be planted at any time, should be pruned as usual in the spring after planting.

Cut back the shoots and roots of bare root roses before planting.

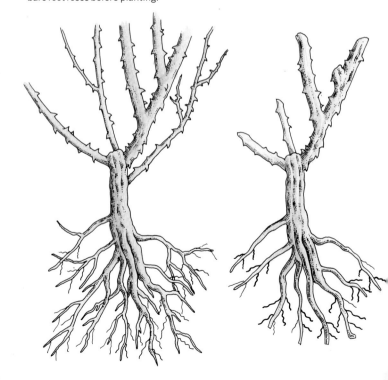

STANDARD ROSES

Both floribundas and hybrid tea roses can be budded at the top of stems 76–122 cm (2½–4 ft) tall instead of at ground level. The main stem should be kept completely free of growth so any shoots should be rubbed out as soon as they appear. Standard roses should always be staked to prevent damage from wind, and the heads need to be kept fairly small, well balanced and open. Make each cut above an outward facing bud so that the shoots will grow away from the centre of the head. Cut back to three buds (hybrid teas) or five buds (floribundas).

WEEPING STANDARDS

These are rambler roses grafted on to 1.8–2.1 m (6–7 ft) tall stems in the same way as other standards, but the lax growth results in an attractive weeping appearance. Keep the head fairly open and well balanced. Prune by cutting out all the shoots that have flowered and retaining the previous season's growth for flowering the coming year. If this leaves too few shoots for an adequate display, a little of the old wood can be utilised by cutting back laterals to two or three buds. To help maintain the shape, tie the young shoots into a wire training frame.

Standard Rose — remove any growth from the stem. Keep the centre open.

HYBRID TEA ROSES (Large Flowered).

This type of rose tends to produce relatively small numbers of large, shapely flowers, often with a strong scent. They flower from early June until the arrival of severe frosts.

Choose a plant with at least three well spaced shoots, and if it is planted during the winter or early spring cut it back in spring, leaving two to four buds. Always try and cut to an outward facing bud to keep the centre of the plant open. In following years prune hybrid teas as soon as they start to grow in spring. Cut out any dead or diseased wood which may be distinguished by black or purple spots or patches on the bark. Always remove any particularly weak growth since this will probably not flower, and inward growing or crossing branches.

The ideal shape for a hybrid tea is relatively open so that the air can circulate freely. This helps reduce the risk of mildew. The remaining strong growth should be cut back to four to six buds, and any weaker shoots rather harder. In later years, one or two pieces of the oldest wood (this has darker, rougher bark) can be cut out at the base.

Hybrid Tea Rose
(Large Flowered)
Cut back to an outward-facing bud.

Popular Cultivars
Silver Jubilee
Grandpa Dixon
Peace
Red Devil
Wendy Cussons

FLORIBUNDA ROSES (Cluster Flowered).

This type of rose produces smaller flowers but makes up for this by carrying them in large clusters right through the summer months making a very impressive garden display.

Generally floribunda roses should be pruned less hard than hybrid teas as they are more vigorous. They make more shapely plants if they are cut back on planting to three to five buds. Choose a plant with at least three strong shoots for these will form a good framework. During the following years cut out any dead, diseased, weak or crossing shoots, and reduce the remaining shoots to six or eight buds. Cut the weaker shoots back much harder to two or three buds. In all pruning, make each cut just above a growth bud. Always remove any leaves or stems which have been blackened by frost. In later years the oldest branches can be cut out entirely.

Popular Cultivars
Iceberg
Evelyn Fison
Queen Elizabeth
City of Leeds
Southampton

Floribunda Rose
(Cluster Flowered)
Keep the centre open.

SHRUB ROSES

There are large numbers of shrub and species roses and these could be further divided into smaller groups and different pruning methods recommended for each. Good results, though, can be had if the guidelines below are followed.

1. On planting, cut out weak and badly placed shoots and tip back the remainder.
2. Regularly dead-head all roses once the flowers have faded, provided they are not grown for their hips.
3. Concentrate on building up a strong framework of sturdy shoots. This can be steadily renewed over the years by cutting out one or two of the oldest branches at the base to leave a fairly open plant.
4. Tip back all vigorous shoots and laterals.
5. Regularly remove all weak, dead, diseased and crossing growth.
6. The species rose, *Rosa rubrifolia,* often grown for its grey-purple leaves, can be cut back fairly hard in spring if desired.
7. Always take account of the flowering habit of the plant so that pruning can be adjusted accordingly.

Popular Cultivars
Handel
Golden Showers
Pink Perpetue
Danse du Feu
Marigold

CLIMBING ROSES

Climbers, unlike Ramblers, will often bloom continuously throughout the summer. The aim, as far as pruning is concerned, is to build up a permanent framework of branches which are tied in securely to fence, wall or post. In the spring after planting, trim off any weak tips and small laterals before training the shoots – there should be three or four – evenly across the allotted space into a fan shape. As the new shoots grow they should also be tied in and the framework established. These branches should be retained as long as they are productive, and their laterals cut back to two or three buds every spring. Strong new shoots will appear periodically but these are usually not produced from the base; they can, though, be used to replace the oldest upper growth or to extend the framework. To encourage new growth from lower down, one of the oldest growths can be cut back hard. If the shoots can be trained horizontally this will help encourage buds towards the base to produce shoots.

RAMBLING ROSES

Ramblers are supple-stemmed compared with the stiff growth of climbers, and ideal for training over pillars. They are rather prone to mildew when grown against walls because of poor air circulation. They usually have only one flowering period in mid-summer, and the large trusses of flowers are born on laterals produced from the previous year's shoots. These shoots usually spring freely from the base of the plant and pruning consists of cutting out all the shoots that have produced flowers, and training in the new growth. If there are not enough new shoots then the strongest of the old ones can be retained, and the laterals cut back to two or three buds. Strong basal growth can be encouraged by feeding with a good rose fertiliser, mulching and watering well during the summer months.

Popular Cultivars
Albertine
Alberic Barbier
Lawrence Johnston
Easleas Golden Rambler

Crimson Shower
Mme. Gregoire Staechlin
François Juranville
Elegance
American Piller

MINIATURE ROSES

These tiny plants usually require little pruning, but they should be trimmed back slightly on planting and any weak growth removed. Dead-heading is important in order to encourage further flowering but in spring, pruning should be relatively light, cutting back to about 15 cm (6 in), and shaping carefully.

Tender micro-roses need less pruning. A trim in spring and regular dead-heading is usually sufficient.

RENOVATION

Sometimes on taking over a new garden you will inherit roses that have been neglected for many years. In the very worst cases where there are large quantities of old wood and dead, diseased and spindly unproductive growth, the rose should be dug up and burnt. If the growth is healthy, however, though not very productive, there are two courses of action you can take.

Remove any dead or weak growth and then cut the remaining shoots back to about 5 cm (2 in) in spring. It is vital that this course of action is combined with a good feed with a rose fertiliser, followed by a generous mulch and plenty of water throughout the following summer months.

The second, more cautious approach is to cut out any dead or diseased wood. Old wood should be cut back to two thirds its length, and any new growth restricted to two buds. This procedure is continued each year until all the old wood is replaced by new. Again, feeding, mulching and watering are vital to the plant's recovery.

FRUIT – TOP FRUIT

APPLES AND PEARS The pruning requirements for apples and pears are broadly similar, although pears usually need cutting back rather harder.

Most cultivars of apples and pears produce their fruits on short lateral growths called spurs. Each spur should produce fruit for many years and the aim of the fruit grower is to produce as large a number of strong spurs as the tree can comfortably bear. Some varieties, such as Bramley's Seedling, fruit towards the tips of the previous year's shoots, and these require a different form of pruning.

The size and cropping ability of a fruit tree is determined by its rootstock, so always consult a reputable nurseryman before buying. For the best results, buy a one-year-old tree, called a maiden, and carry out the necessary training yourself.
Forming a Bush Tree and Spur Pruning Start with a tree with just one shoot and during its dormant period, cut it back to about 60 cm (2 ft). During the second year a number of vigorous shoots will be produced and these should be cut back by about half.

Follow the same procedure the following year but also cut back the laterals to three buds.

In following years, the leaders can be reduced less severely but the laterals must still be cut back to three buds. It is this

Apple – thin out overcrowded spurs

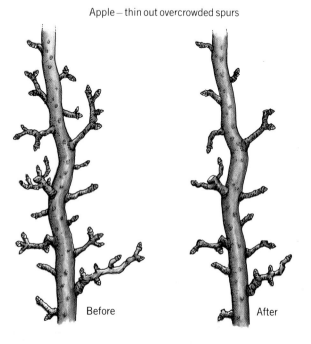

Before   After

shortening of the laterals which encourages the production of fruiting spurs.

Tip Bearers The majority of varieties respond well to spur pruning but tip-bearing types, although sometimes producing reasonable crops when pruned according to the spur system, are best if treated as follows.

Shorten the leaders by about half and cut back *some* of the shoots from the laterals to one bud, leaving the others totally unpruned so that they may bear fruit. Alternatively, as tip-bearing varieties tend to be larger, more vigorous trees, it is sometimes more convenient to simply thin out the whole tree, removing in particular any crowded or crossing branches.

The eventual aim is for an even distribution of branches with an open centre.

Tip bearers are not suitable for growing as cordons.

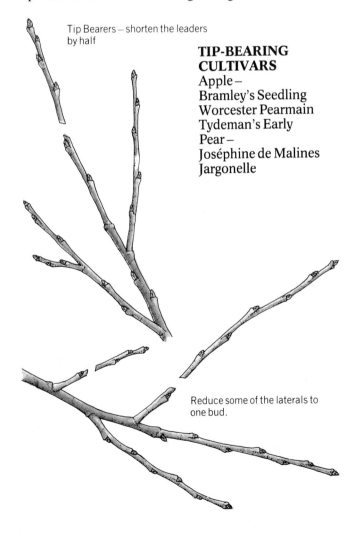

Tip Bearers – shorten the leaders by half

TIP-BEARING CULTIVARS
Apple –
Bramley's Seedling
Worcester Pearmain
Tydeman's Early
Pear –
Joséphine de Malines
Jargonelle

Reduce some of the laterals to one bud.

24

Cordons These are dwarf trees trained on a single stem tied to wires, and usually grown at an angle. Their small size makes them particularly convenient to look after. The fruit can be picked easily, and spraying and pruning can be comfortably carried out without a ladder. Sometimes the trees develop too many spurs, and these may need to be thinned out occasionally.

Once they are established, cordons are best pruned in the summer. In August cut back new laterals from the main stem to 7.5 cm (3 in) while sublaterals – the shoots growing from existing laterals – should be cut back to 2.5 cm (1 in). Summer pruning helps restrain the vigour of the plant, promotes the production of fruit buds and allows light to penetrate so that the fruit can ripen well.

Apple – pruning a cordon.

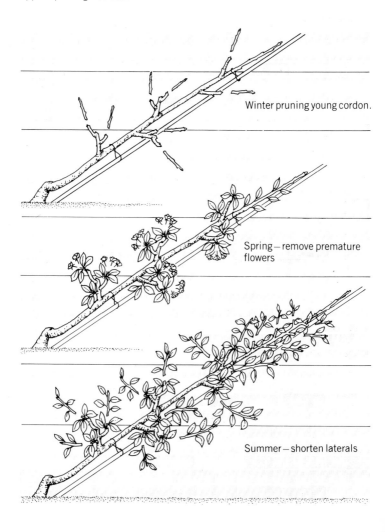

Winter pruning young cordon.

Spring – remove premature flowers

Summer – shorten laterals

Espaliers This is another form of tree with restricted growth. A central stem is trained vertically while tiers of horizontal branches are tied in to wires. Once established, espaliers are summer pruned in exactly the same way as cordons, and in the same manner overcrowded spur systems may need to be thinned in later years. Building up the framework of an espalier takes time and skill but the end result is well worth the amount of work necessary. Some nurseries sell espaliers that are already partly trained, but they tend to be rather expensive.

Apple — training an espalier.

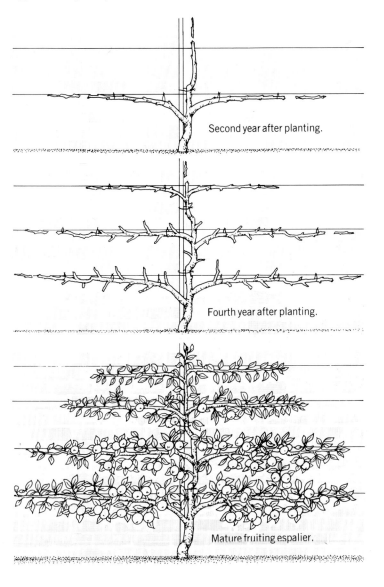

Second year after planting.

Fourth year after planting.

Mature fruiting espalier.

PLUM

This popular fruit, which also includes gages and bullaces, is normally grown as a bush, standard, half-standard or fan. Unfortunately plum trees cannot be grown as cordons or dwarf trees in the same way as apples.

The formation of a good branch structure is vital and correct training must take place in the early stages.

First winter: plant a maiden tree and cut back to 1.5–1.8 m (5–6 ft). Trim any laterals back to 7.5 cm (3 in). During the first summer, strong shoots will grow from the top of the trunk.

Second winter: choose four or five evenly spaced shoots (these will form the main branches) and cut them back by half. Shorten all other growth to 7.5 cm (3 in).

Third winter: retain two shoots on each branch selected the previous winter and cut them back by half. Cut the other shoots back to 7.5 cm (3 in).

During the following years: prune in June–July to help guard against silver leaf, a deadly fungus disease which attacks through pruning cuts in winter. Remove all dead, diseased and crossing wood. Cut back laterals to 7.5 cm (3 in). Suckers may be removed at any time.

DAMSON

Once the branch structure of these trees is established, routine pruning during June or July consists of removing any branches crowding the centre of the tree, together with any dead, diseased or unproductive wood.

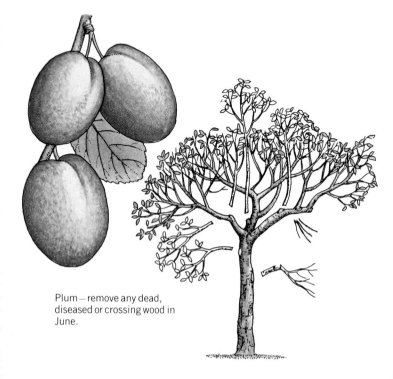

Plum — remove any dead, diseased or crossing wood in June.

SWEET CHERRY
Unfortunately these trees grow very large and since two varieties are needed to ensure pollination (each tree is self-sterile), they are not recommended for small gardens. However, a new, dwarfing rootstock is becoming available and this may soon bring sweet cherries within the range of the average gardener.

The trees can be grown successfully against a wall provided there is enough space. One advantage of this method is that the crops can be protected easily from the birds with netting. Fan training is the most logical system and the framework of the tree can be built up in the same way as that given for peaches, see overleaf.

In July or August, cut out any overcrowded or badly placed branches and pinch back new growth to five leaves. Leaders can be allowed to grow if extension growth is still needed. When the space is filled cut back to a lower lateral. All shoots which grow back against the wall or strong shoots which grow forward should be cut out as soon as they appear. In the autumn all the shoots which were shortened to five leaves should be cut back to three buds. The branches should be tied into the wire during the winter months.

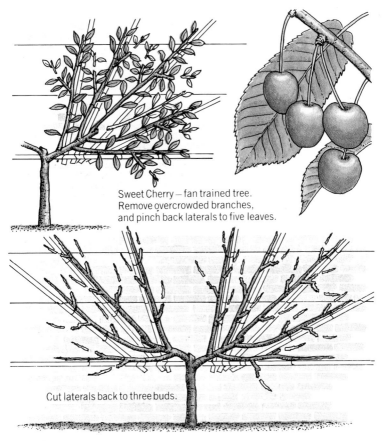

Sweet Cherry — fan trained tree.
Remove overcrowded branches,
and pinch back laterals to five leaves.

Cut laterals back to three buds.

PEACHES AND NECTARINES
Because these trees flower early it is the blossom, rather than the plants themselves, which is tender. To help protect these fragile blooms, peaches and nectarines are usually grown against a south-facing wall or fence.

Pruning is not simple. First build up the framework of a fan trained tree. Both trees fruit on the previous year's growth so the aim is to produce a constant supply of new growth. Shoots that have fruited are removed and replaced with the new shoots which will fruit the following year.

In spring, as the buds burst, select two buds towards the base of the previous year's growth to form the fruiting shoots for next year. Rub out any buds below these.

Allow the terminal bud to produce six leaves then pinch it back to four. As the fruits swell, thin them to about 23 cm (9 in) apart.

Pinch back all shoots where there are fruits to two leaves, and the others to about 2.5 cm (1 in). Select which of the two basal shoots is best placed in relation to other branches, and cut out the other.

After fruiting, cut the branch that has fruited back to its replacement.

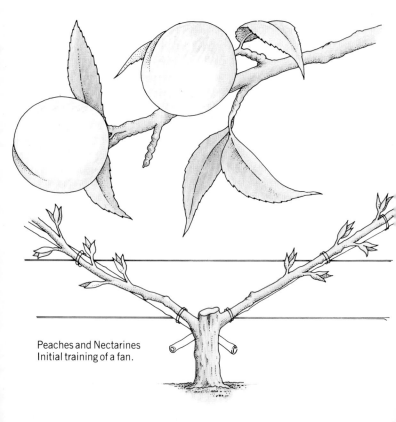

Peaches and Nectarines
Initial training of a fan.

MORELLO CHERRY

These fruit in much the same way as peaches and if trained as a fan tree can be pruned in a similar way. Some varieties do not produce strong replacement shoots readily, so a proportion of the older growth may need to be cut back hard. Morellos can also be grown as ordinary trees in the same way as plums, in which case pruning consists of cutting older shoots back to one-year-old laterals in spring. If there are only a few laterals some of the previous year's shoots may need to be cut back to 7.5–10 cm (3–4 in) as well.

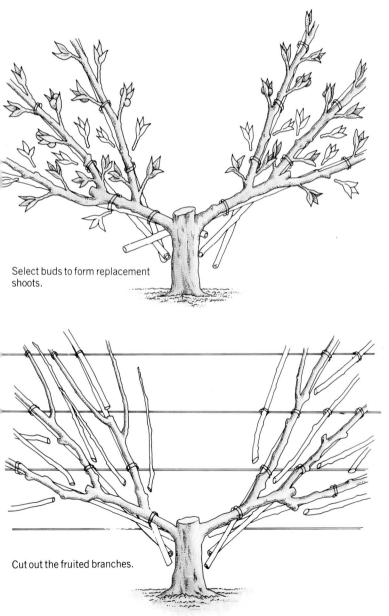

Select buds to form replacement shoots.

Cut out the fruited branches.

SOFT FRUIT

RASPBERRY This has a characteristic habit of growth which is shared by blackberries and loganberries. Instead of forming a basic branch structure that persists from year to year, strong growths are made each year from below ground, so unless regular pruning is carried out each year, the result is an impenetrable and sparsely fruiting thicket.

Summer fruiting raspberries produce fruit on short laterals from the canes produced during the previous year. Autumn fruiting varieties produce raspberries on the current season's growth. Always plant canes which are certified virus-free. Plant new canes about 60 cm (2 ft) apart during the winter months

Raspberry – cut out old canes after fruiting.

and cut them down to 23 cm (9 in). New shoots will appear in the spring and when these are growing well the old cane stumps can be removed completely. Tie the canes to horizontal wires as they grow.

Make sure all the canes are tied in well by the winter, and in the spring cut the tips back to 15 cm (6 in) above the top wire. Laterals will be produced during the spring which will flower and fruit, and at the same time strong new shoots will appear from the base. Select enough to provide one cane every 7.5–10 cm (3–4 in) and remove the others. After fruiting, all the canes that have produced a crop should be cut out at ground level and the new canes tied in.

Autumn fruiting varieties should be cut down to 23 cm (9 in) on planting, and cut down to ground level each spring. During late spring, thin out the weakest shoots leaving the strongest canes to grow on.

Cut autumn-fruiting varieties to ground level in spring.

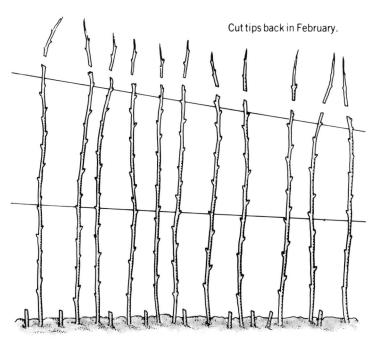

Cut tips back in February.

GOOSEBERRY

Many people are reluctant to prune gooseberries – possibly because of the thorns – and the result is a tangled mass of growth with fruit that is almost impossible to pick without getting badly scratched. Building up a sturdy branch structure with many fruiting spurs and adequate space between the branches is probably the best way to get good crops of fruit which can be picked in relative comfort. Plant between November and February when the bushes are dormant. Cut back the side shoots by about half. As gooseberries have a tendency to 'flop' cut to an inward facing bud. During the following winter, select about six shoots to form the branch structure, and cut these back by half. The remaining shoots can be cut back to 7 cm (3 in). Continue in this manner each winter.

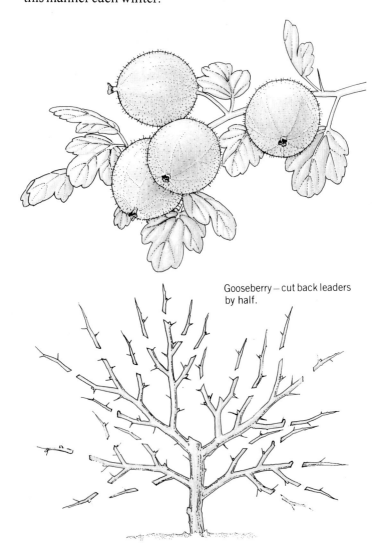

Gooseberry – cut back leaders by half.

BLACK CURRANT

When you buy your first black currant bush you need to be brave, for having planted it, in winter or early spring, you must cut the branches back very hard, leaving only 2.5–5 cm (1–2 in) with no more than two buds. (However, the healthy young shoots can be used as cuttings, so all is not lost.) During the following year these buds will produce vigorous shoots which will form the basis for future crops. If the shoots are pruned less severely on planting, or worse still, if they are not pruned at all, a large amount of weaker growth will be made, and this is the last thing you need if you want the bushes to produce good, heavy crops.

Black currants fruit on shoots that have grown during the previous season, so although weak new shoots can be cut out at the base, the others should not be pruned at all. These shoots will fruit the following summer.

In the following years, pruning consists of removing about one half to a third of the oldest wood each year, as low down on the plant as possible. Weak twigs and damaged or diseased wood should also be cut out, together with any particularly low branches from which the fruit may rub on the ground and become damaged.

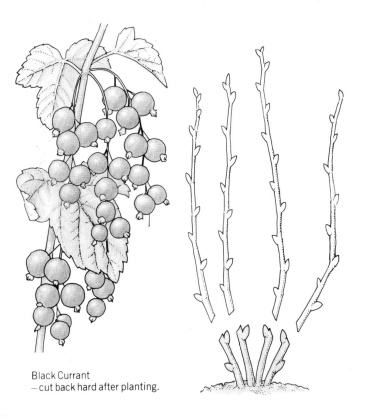

Black Currant
– cut back hard after planting.

RED AND WHITE CURRANTS

Both these fruits can be grown on short legs, as cordons or even as a dividing hedge between the fruit and vegetable garden. Red and white currants fruit on short spurs borne on the previous season's wood. When pruning, the aim should be to construct a strong spur system. In the early years build up a framework of between eight and ten permanent branches. The fruiting spurs can be encouraged to form by shortening all laterals to five leaves in summer, and in winter by cutting back the leaders by about half. As the plant matures the leaders will have to be cut back even more, and eventually reduced to 2.5 cm (1 in). The oldest dark wood can be cut back hard and new shoots from low down should be trained in to take its place. Unfortunately red and white currants suffer from gall mite and reversion virus in the same way as black currants.

Red and White Currant – cut back the leaders by half, and the laterals to two buds.

Shorten resulting growth to five leaves.

BLACKBERRY

BLACKBERRY The cultivated varieties bear much bigger and sweeter fruits than the wild blackberries found in the hedgerows. Blackberries fruit on laterals growing from shoots made the previous year. Other related fruits which are pruned in the same way include the loganberry, boysenberry, Japanese wineberry, thornless loganberry and veitchberry.

Young blackberry plants should be cut back to 23 cm (9 in) when planting in the winter. The training in future years should stem from the fact that most blackberries are both vigorous and thorny, and if each year's growth can be kept separate it will help enormously. Blackberries should be trained on supporting wires with all the new growth trained along the wires to one side of the root only. Any damaged tips on these shoots can be lightly tipped back in early spring. These canes are the ones which will bear fruit, and at the same time a new crop of canes will appear from the base – these should be trained along the wires in the opposite direction.

After fruiting the old canes are cut out at the base and so it goes on, alternating pruning from one side to the other.

Blackberry – cut out the old canes immediately after fruiting.

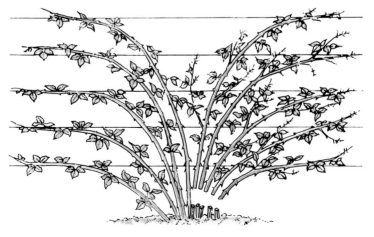

SHRUBS

Shrubs flower on *three* different types of shoot and, as far as pruning is concerned, each group is treated differently. The first group of summer-flowering plants, such as Buddleia, Caryopteris and Fuchsia, produce their flowers on growth made in the earlier part of the same year, also referred to as the current season's growth. They are pruned in late winter or early spring to encourage strong new growths to shoot from just below the pruning cut, and these shoots flower later in the year.

The second group of plants flower on the shoots that have grown during the previous year, which is also referred to as the previous season's wood. These include Forsythia, Philadelphus (Mock Orange) and Weigela. Unlike the first group, these shrubs must *not* be pruned in late winter, as the wood you would be cutting out is that bearing all the flower buds. The shrubs in this group are pruned *after* flowering. Once the flowers fade, cut out all the shoots that have borne flowers.

The third, and much smaller group, includes Chaenomeles (Japanese Quince) and Wisteria which flower, like apple trees,

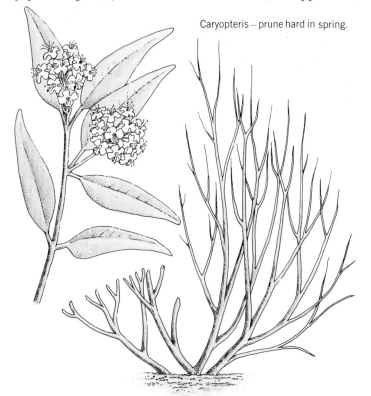

Caryopteris — prune hard in spring.

on spurs. That is, the flowers are produced from the same short, stubby growths every year. These spurs can be encouraged by shortening new growth in summer, and nipping back the resultant side shoots later in the year. Some shoots can be retained to increase the size or improve the shape of the plant.

Not all shrubs require annual pruning, so check the individual requirements of each plant before you start.

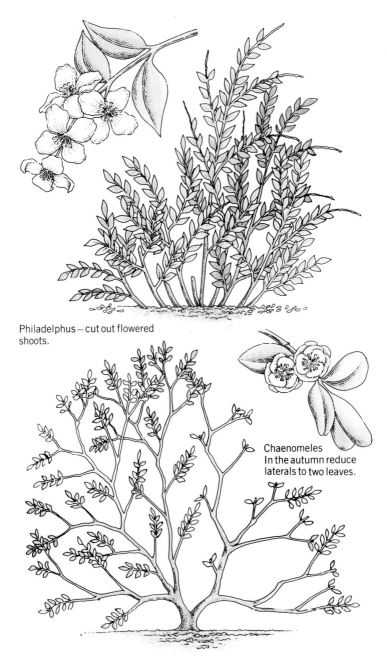

Philadelphus — cut out flowered shoots.

Chaenomeles
In the autumn reduce laterals to two leaves.

CLIMBERS & WALL PLANTS

The pruning guidelines for established climbing plants are exactly the same as those for shrubs. As before, the timing is dictated by the method of flowering, i.e. on the current season's growth, the previous year's growth, or on spurs. With climbers, however, the amount of space available may be critical.

Climbers which are planted to grow through trees are generally best left unpruned, both for practical purposes and safety reasons. Climbers which are planted against walls or fences should be tied in to a system of horizontal wires and the early growths trained in to a fan shape.

Supporting canes are first tied to the wires and the shoots in turn are tied to the canes. Lateral shoots can be tied in to the wires. As the wall or fence area becomes more densely covered some thinning may be necessary, particularly if the growth is uneven. Try to keep the base of the plant well furnished with branches. Vigorous, self-supporting climbers such as clematis must be trained initially as it is difficult to remove the clinging growth once it has a hold. The young shoots of Ivies (Hedera) also need training against their supporting fence or wall.

Key – Group 1 – Flower on the current season's growth
Group 2 – Flower on the previous season's growth
Group 3 – Flower on spurs

CLEMATIS (1 & 2)
Clematis can be divided into two groups, those that flower in spring and early summer on the previous year's shoots and those that flower in late summer and early autumn on growth made the same year.

Spring and early summer flowering Clematis include the following: *C. montana, C. macropetala, C.* 'Nelly Moser', *C.* 'Vyvyan Pennell', *C.* 'The President' and *C.* 'Lasurstern'.

These should be pruned immediately the flowers are over. Remove as much of the flowered growth as possible, and thin out any tangled wood and shoots. If varieties in this group get out of hand they can be cut back very hard as they start into growth in spring, although the flowers for that year will be lost.

Late summer and early autumn flowering Clematis include *C. x jackmanii, C.* 'Ville de Lyon', *C.* 'Ernest Markham', *C.* 'Hagley Hybrid', *C.* 'Henryi', *C.* 'Comtesse de Bouchaud'.

These can be cut back hard in spring just as growth is beginning. If the plants are left unpruned, or only shortened slightly, the flowers will mainly appear high up on the plant leaving the lower stems bare. Cutting shoots to various lengths, from 15 cm (6 in) to 90 cm (3 ft), will ensure coverage of a greater height of wall.

WISTERIA (3)

Wisterias are vigorous growers and should not be planted in a confined space where they will have to be unnaturally restricted. However, if left completely unpruned they will soon reach the roof of the house and dislodge the tiles with their invasive shoots, causing considerable damage. In spite of being such a vigorous plant, Wisterias can sometimes be very slow starters. Cut the young plant back by about half on planting to encourage strong basal growth, from which to train the basic framework. Spur pruning is then practised and the lateral shoots are cut back to 15 cm (6 in) in July except for any shoots needed to extend the framework.

In winter these shoots should be cut back to two buds to encourage the plant to produce large drooping racemes of flowers in the following spring.

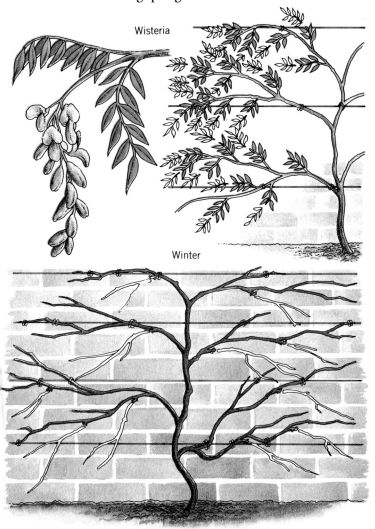

Wisteria

Winter

TREES

TREE TRAINING Trees are the largest and most important plants in the garden and because of their long lifespan, it is important that they should be well shaped from the beginning. Pruning, particularly in the early stages, is a vital factor in forming a well shaped tree.

Basically, there are two types of tree: the feathered tree and the standard tree. The feathered tree has branches almost down to ground level, while the standard tree has a clear trunk of about 1.5–1.8 m (5–6 ft) before the first branch. In both cases the aim should be for a strong evenly spaced branch structure.

If feathered trees are planted round the edge of a lawn, the lowest branches may be removed (always cut them flush with the main trunk). This not only makes grass cutting easier, but the lower branches are not damaged by the lawn mower.

THINNING A DENSE TREE Deciduous trees planted close to windows sometimes cast too much shade and may need thinning. Although it is easier to see in summer, by the amount of shade cast, which branches need removing, an even branch structure is more easily attained if pruning is done in winter when the tree has shed its leaves. Perhaps the best plan is to mark in summer the branches which seem to need removal and then to do the pruning in the winter when the overall branch structure can be seen.

Thinning should only be attempted on small trees providing the necessary work is easily managed. For larger specimens, always enlist the help of a specialist – it is safer for both you and the tree. On a smallish tree, up to half the branches can be removed without undue harm, but do make sure that all wounds are sealed with protective wound paint as soon as the cuts are made. Conifers are best left unpruned and unthinned, although some varieties such as x *Cupressocyparis leylandii* will stand clipping.

TOPIARY The art of training evergreens such as yew and box into unnatural shapes belongs more to the days of grand houses and formal gardens, although many exotic creations can also be seen throughout the countryside, often in cottage gardens. The animals or birds are made by tying selected branches to a wire framework, and by careful clipping. Any branches which would ruin the shape are removed completely. With care and patience the most fantastic shapes can be created, but they do need constant attention if their neat shape is to be retained.

SMALL SCALE SURGERY

Repairs When it comes to tree surgery the first rule is not to be too ambitious. Scrambling about high in the branches of an old tree is sheer folly and could have a disastrous end. If major work is necessary, for example, the felling of dead elms, it is much easier *and* safer, to call in an expert. There are, however, some tasks that can safely be undertaken by the gardener, and in particular routine work on dwarf fruit trees and the less vigorous flowering trees which are suitable for the small garden.

Broken branches are one of the commonest troubles and can arise from storm damage, a misdirected football, or maybe a child swinging on a thin branch. Sadly it is usually a waste of time to try and splice the two pieces together. The majority of these breaks are usually rough tears which trap water and cause the affected part to rot. It is far better to remove the damaged wood and cut back to a lower branch or shoot which can be trained in as a replacement.

Suckers These should always be removed as they are both unsightly and an unnecessary drain on the tree's resources. Cherries, limes, and various weeping trees are particularly prone to suckering. Always remove suckers as close as possible to their point of origin.

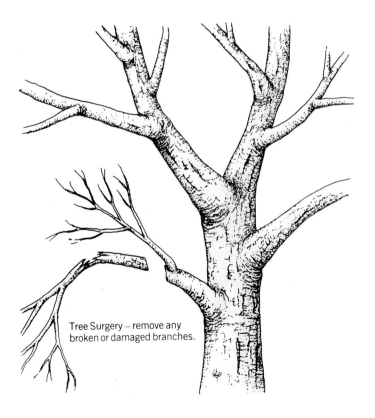

Tree Surgery — remove any
broken or damaged branches.

HEDGES

A good hedge, whatever its type and use, is formed largely by its early training. For example, if you allow a hedge to reach its required height too quickly, without cutting it back, it will soon become bare at the base and thin in the middle. Constant cutting back encourages the thick bushy growth which makes the hedge an impenetrable barrier.

With the exception of conifers, cut back all hedging plants by half after planting. Upright growing subjects like privet (Ligustrum) and snowberry (Symphoricarpos) can be cut back by half or even more, while those tending to form a trunk, like beech (Fagus) and hornbeam (Carpinus) should be cut back by only a third.

In the following year trim privet and snowberry lightly in midsummer and in winter cut back by about a third. Thereafter trim to shape as required. Beeches should not be touched again until the following winter when all growth can be cut back by a quarter or a third. Trimming to shape can begin in the following year.

Flowering hedges are best treated informally, that is left to grow freely, and should be cut at the appropriate pruning time, depending on their flowering season.

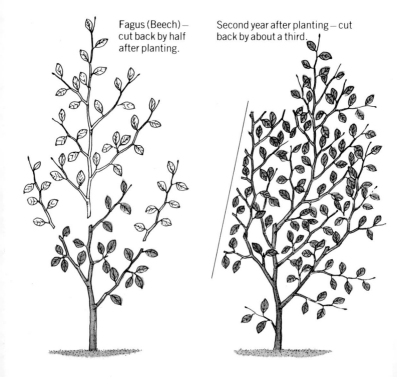

Fagus (Beech) — cut back by half after planting.

Second year after planting — cut back by about a third.

Conifer hedging should be allowed to grow until the required height is reached. The top is then cut 15 cm (6 in) below the final height and the sides lightly trimmed.

Established hedges should be trimmed so that they are wider at the base, tapering slightly to a flat top. This helps keep the base well covered, and makes the hedge more resistant to snow and strong winds.

Large-leaved hedging plants should always be trimmed with secateurs, for if the leaves themselves are cut, not only will they look ugly but the edges will turn brown and die. Electric or hand trimmers are, of course, fine for small-leaved plants, and the more often such a hedge is clipped, the more formal the appearance.

Small hedges which are used more to mark the edges of borders, rather than the edges of gardens, can be cut square, but no hedge should ever be cut with the top wider than the bottom.

CHEMICAL PRUNING

Cutting hedges, especially long ones, can be a tiresome business. Vigorous hedges like Privet are especially troublesome and a useful labour-saving device is a chemical which can be sprayed on the hedge to suppress the growth. Although the apical bud growth is suppressed, the spray encourages all the lateral buds to break slowly so that the hedge grows less but becomes more bushy. The hedge is cut normally and a short time after the growth regulator is sprayed on. The slow-growth effect of the chemical lasts for a whole season.

Berberis x stenophylla — clip into shape immediately after flowering.

Before

After

Pruning Calendar

The times indicated in this pruning calendar are intended as a rough guide only, for the climate can vary by as much as three weeks from one part of the country to another.

JANUARY Overhaul garden equipment and tools. Brush snow off conifers and other evergreens. Remove any damaged or broken branches .

FEBRUARY Complete winter pruning of apples, pears and bush fruits. Remove any dead wood or suckers. Cut autumn fruiting raspberries to ground level.
Start pruning plants grown in the greenhouse.

MARCH Prune established roses. Cut back hard any shrubs grown for their decorative foliage or coloured stems. Any shrubs which need rejuvenating should also be cut back hard. Cut out the old fronds from ferns. Prune Buddleias and other shrubs which flower on the current season's growth.

APRIL Start pruning shrubs which flower on the previous year's growth as the flowers begin to fade. Clip over winter heathers after the flowers fade.

MAY Dead-head Rhododendrons. Remove any rose suckers. Start clipping hedges. Continue pruning spring-flowering shrubs.

JUNE Pinch out growing tips of bedding plants after planting. Pinch out Dahlias and Chrysanthemums as necessary. Continue pruning spring-flowering shrubs. Prune Plum trees.

JULY Thin out Apples if necessary now that the natural 'drop' is over. Prune Cherry trees. Prune Red and White Currants.

AUGUST Dead-head Buddleias and other summer-flowering shrubs plus herbaceous plants and annuals. Summer prune Wisteria, Apples and other fruits. Clip conifer hedges. Prune Cordon Apples and Pears.

SEPTEMBER Thin Grapes. Cut out old Raspberry canes. Prune Peach trees after the fruit is harvested.

OCTOBER Start pruning top fruit after leaf fall. Cut out old canes from blackberries and hybrid berries.

NOVEMBER Cut back Roses and Buddleias by half to prevent wind rock. Start pruning Black Currants and Gooseberries.

DECEMBER Prune Vines. Root prune top fruits and Figs if necessary. Spur back Chaenomeles and Wisteria.

GUIDE TO A HEALTHY GARDEN

No garden is perfect, and however hard you try to grow pest-
and disease-free plants, sooner or later your cherished beauties
are going to be attacked by some beast or blight that does its
best to wipe out your good work. If you and your plants are to
survive the onslaught then something has to be done to combat
the enemy.

By far the best protection at your disposal is common sense,
coupled with observation. With the wide range of chemicals
available to the gardener nowadays, it is easy to develop a sense
of hypochondria and to storm out into the garden with a
sprayer at the first sign of a greenfly. While prevention is
certainly better than cure, the wise gardener will consider
carefully his course of action rather than rushing like a bull at a
gate towards the problem.

If chemicals are found to be the only solution, the most
appropriate product should be sought out and applied in
accordance with the manufacturer's instructions. Really
common diseases like rose mildew and blackspot are almost
bound to recur year after year, and it is sensible to spray the
plants even before the diseases appear to prevent them from
gaining a foothold. Other less widespread pests and diseases
need be tackled only when they start to get out of hand, but
some are so vicious that instant remedial action is necessary;
this book will help you to differentiate between minor
problems and disasters.

When a pest or disease problem baffles you, don't be afraid to
ask for advice. Local gardening societies, knowledgeable
neighbours and allotment holders, and even the Royal
Horticultural Society's Garden at Wisley in Surrey (if you are a
member) are usually willing to help out, and the national
gardening magazines also run a consultancy service.

But before you go to these lengths, read through the pages of
this book. All the most common pests, diseases and disorders
have been described for flowers, fruits and vegetables, and it
should not be too difficult for you to locate your problem and
take the measures necessary to protect your plants. Whether
you grow fruits, vegetables or flowers, the preparation of the
ground they are to grow in is vitally important.

Always dig new soil thoroughly, removing weeds, large
stones and any builders' debris. Nearly all plants will benefit if
some kind of organic enrichment is incorporated into the soil.
Use well-rotted garden compost, manure, spent hops, spent
mushroom compost or, as a last resort, peat mixed with a
little general fertiliser to help it rot down and to improve its
nutrient value.

General fertilisers such as growmore, and blood, bone and fish meal, applied at two handfuls to 0.83 m² (1 sq yd), can be scattered on to the soil around plants in spring and lightly hoed in to give them a boost and to replace nutrients washed out by winter rains.

Through the summer, liquid foliar feeds can be sprayed on to plant leaves – they are easily absorbed and go quickly into action. Apply any fertiliser or liquid feed in accordance with the manufacturer's instructions; do not add one for the pot – it may do more harm than good.

Avoid applying food or fertiliser to plants outdoors after September, for this may encourage sappy growth which cannot withstand frosts.

In prolonged dry spells plants should be thoroughly watered (especially those plants which have shallow root systems and those which have been newly planted). Leave a hosepipe and sprinkler running over the piece of ground for at least an hour to ensure adequate water penetration. Light sprays that dampen the surface of the soil will encourage the formation of surface roots which may perish in drought.

Once soil is moist, a 5 cm (2 in) thick 'mulch' of coarse peat, pulverised bark or leafmould can be spread over the surface to keep in moisture and suppress weeds.

Few plants will grow in soil that is waterlogged or excessively shaded, so ensure that drainage is efficient and light adequate.

LIGHT AND TEMPERATURE
Unless shade-loving plants are being grown a well-lit site should be chosen. Plants manufacture their food with the aid of sunlight and will become spindly and pale if they are deprived of this energy. They will function very slowly in cold spots, and may wilt or sustain leaf damage on windy sites. Plants do not start to grow until temperatures rise above 6°C (43°F), so cold sites mean a late start to the spring and a delay in seed sowing.

Areas at the foot of slopes collect cold air and are generally known as frost pockets. You should avoid planting in them any plants that are susceptible to very low temperatures and spring frosts.

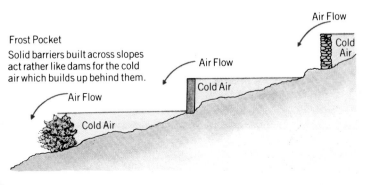

Frost Pocket
Solid barriers built across slopes act rather like dams for the cold air which builds up behind them.

Air Flow
Cold Air
Air Flow
Cold Air
Air Flow
Cold Air

DISEASE RESISTANCE
To give your plants the best chance of avoiding attack by pests and diseases, you should make sure that they are healthy at the outset, whether bought in from a nursery or supplied by a friend or neighbour.

When you receive a plant, check that its leaves are healthy and not mottled or distorted (usually a sign of virus infection). Never propagate from virus-infected plants, and never allow them to remain in your garden. Pull them up and burn them (don't compost them or the infection may be spread). Viruses are usually carried and spread by aphids (greenfly) so by keeping these under control you are on the way to stamping out the likelihood of a virus attack.

Plants such as strawberries, seed potatoes and raspberry canes can be bought certified virus free. They will cost a little more with this guarantee, but the extra expense is well worth while, for viruses not only reduce the vigour of plants but reduce their cropping ability too.

Healthy, well-grown plants that have ample supplies of food and water show a natural resistance to more pests and diseases than plants which are weak and hungry. There are also plants which have been specially bred to show resistance to particular diseases. Potato varieties such as Maris Peer and Pentland Crown will resist attacks by potato blight; Arran Pilot and King Edward are resistant to scab. Many new antirrhinum varieties are resistant to the disfiguring rust disease, and certain varieties of lettuce will resist downy mildew.

HYGIENE
Just as in the kitchen, where hygiene is necessary to avoid food poisoning, hygiene in the garden will remove the risk of attack by many plant enemies. Clear up all fallen leaves and debris which can act as hiding places for slugs – they particularly enjoy the collection of rubbish in hedge bottoms.

Weeds are attacked by the same pests as many vegetables, so pull them up and keep the ground clean.

In the greenhouse hygiene is especially important. Try to scrub down the inside of the house at least once a year to kill any pests and overwintering eggs which may be sheltering in cracks and crevices. Always use sterilised composts and clean trays and pots to prevent seedlings and plants from being attacked by fungal diseases.

In the garden all waste should be disposed of thoughtfully. Woody prunings should be burned on domestic fires or (as a last resort) bonfires, and any green plant matter composted so that it can be rotted down and returned to the soil. The following materials can be put on the compost heap:
Lawn mowings, annual weeds, potato peelings, cabbage stalks, green tops of all crops, tea-leaves, crushed eggshells, small amounts of shredded newspaper. (Make sure that all the materials are mixed and that there is no concentration of one particular substance in any one place in the heap.)

USING CHEMICALS

It is important that the most effective chemical is applied when it will be most successful in controlling the pest or disease. The following chart gives a rough idea of how the treatment varies.

PEST OR DISEASE	CATEGORY	DAMAGE	TYPE OF CHEMICAL	TIMING
Aphids (greenfly)	Insect	Sap sucked	Systemic insecticide (travels in sap stream)	As soon as seen
Birds	—	Leaves/fruits eaten & torn	Deterrent	As soon as plant becomes susceptible but before attack
Caterpillars	Insect	Leaves eaten	Contact insecticide (kills insects it touches when sprayed)	As soon as seen but before severe damage is done
Damping-off in seedlings	Fungus	Seedlings keel over & die	Fungicide	As soon as seedlings emerge and before fungus attacks
Mildew	Fungus	Leaves and stems colonised and weakened	Systemic fungicide (travels short distance in sap stream)	Spring—before disease is seen.
Peach leaf curl	Fungus	Leaves distorted; plant weakened	Systemic fungicide	When buds start to swell in winter
Rabbits/deer	Mammals	Plants eaten; trees ring-barked	Deterrent	Before damage is seen if animals known to be present
Slugs	Molluscs	Plants eaten	Poisoned bait or traps	Before damage is seen if pests known to be present
Soil pests (grubs)	Insects	Roots and stems eaten	Soil insecticide dusts or granules applied to soil	At sowing or planting if grubs known to be present
Virus diseases	—	Plants deformed and discoloured; generally weakened	NONE	DESTROY AS SOON AS SEEN

CHEMICAL FORMULATIONS

The method of application of a pesticide or fungicide will depend on the form in which it is sold. The following are the most common formulations:

Sprays Liquids or soluble powders, both of which should be diluted in water, are the most common type of garden chemical. They should be applied either with a hand sprayer or a pump-up pressurised sprayer or, in some cases, a watering can fitted with a fine sprinkler head.

Aerosols Aerosol cans of ready-mixed spray are more expensive than chemicals which need diluting but they are handy and safer where small numbers of plants are to be treated. They should always be shaken before use, and held at least 30 cm (1 ft) away from the plant while spraying. The empty can should not be punctured.

Dusts Usually supplied in plastic 'puffer-packs', chemical dusts should be applied to plants so that a thin film coats the foliage. Their disadvantage is that they are visible and make plants look rather dirty.

Granules These are usually used as slow-release soil insecticides. They can be scattered on the soil from a pepper-pot type of dispenser. Soil insecticide dusts can also be supplied in this type of container. Some foliar insecticides are now sold in the form of water-soluble granules.

Baits Slug pellets usually consist of a tempting carrier (such as bran) treated with a poison. A few of them should be grouped together and protected from rain and animals with pieces of slate or tile.

Fumigants Greenhouse pests can be controlled with smoke pellets or canisters. Close the house down, light the pellet or canister (like a firework) and then leave to smoulder all night. In the morning open and ventilate the greenhouse.

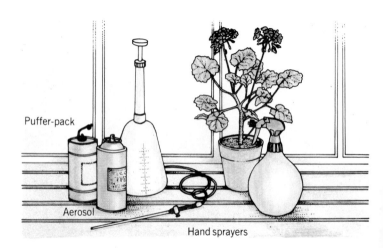

Puffer-pack

Aerosol

Hand sprayers

SAFETY PRECAUTIONS

When dealing with garden chemicals it is essential that certain precautions be taken to prevent children, wild animals and pets from being harmed. The user, too, should treat the formulations with respect.

1. READ THE INSTRUCTIONS ON THE CONTAINER AND FOLLOW THEM TO THE LETTER. DO NOT ADD ONE FOR THE POT.

2. Always wear rubber gloves when handling undiluted chemicals. Wash your hands and face afterwards.

3. Spray at the time indicated on the container, and also at the recommended intervals.

4. Spray in the evening or on dull days when bees and pollinating insects are not active.

5. Mix only as much spray as you can use. Flush surplus amounts of spray down the lavatory and dispose of empty containers by capping them tightly, wrapping them in a polythene bag and placing them in the dustbin.

6. Always use hand sprayers which are kept specifically for insecticide and fungicide application.

7. Do not spray garden chemicals on windy days or in bright sunshine, and do not spray into open flowers.

8. Store all chemicals in their original containers in a secure cupboard out of the reach of children and pets.

9. When spraying edible crops, always allow the recommended interval to elapse before harvesting.

10. Always wash all fruits and vegetables before eating.

VEGETABLES

Pests and diseases find vegetables easy to attack because they are grown in large numbers within a confined space. Crop rotation helps to keep problems to a minimum, but there are certain pests which attack a wide range of crops and these can be controlled as follows:

Aphids Greenfly, blackfly and their relatives (some of which are pinkish-red in colour) are easily killed by spraying with a specific aphicide such as ICI Rapid Greenfly Killer (which will not harm ladybirds, lacewings and bees), or with a general systemic insecticide such as Murphy Systemic Insecticide, Boots Systemic Greenfly Killer, or Bio Systemic Insecticide. Repeat at intervals recommended on the container.

Slugs Slugs can be killed by poisoned bait placed under a propped-up tile or slate adjacent to susceptible plants. The slug pellets need to be replenished when they become wet and soggy, and should always be kept out of reach of animals. May & Baker Draza Slug Pellets, and pbi Slug Gard are both suitable. If pets and garden animals are felt to be at risk, slug traps should be constructed. Sink an old yogurt carton into the soil, its rim level with the surface, and fill with beer. In the morning empty out the slugs and snails which will have crawled in overnight and died in the heady brew.

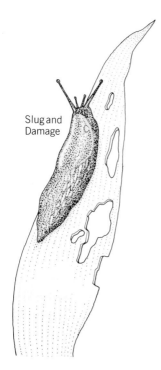

Slug and Damage

Birds Brassicas in particular can be decimated by pigeons. Keep these and other birds off crops by covering the plants completely with plastic netting held over a framework of canes. Some spray-on bird deterrents will last longer than others. Garotta's Scoot and Synchemicals' Stay Off are particularly durable, and should deter birds for up to six weeks, depending on the weather.

BROAD BEAN
Grow on soils that have been manured for a previous crop. Good drainage is essential.

PROBLEMS

Blackfly *Dense clusters of small black insects on shoot tips.* CURE: Prevent by pinching out shoot tips as soon as five clusters of flowers have formed. Spray bad infestations with ICI Rapid Greenfly Killer; Boots Greenfly Killer, or Murphy Liquid Malathion.

Pea & Bean Weevil *Edges of leaves scalloped.* CURE: Tolerate if plants are mature. Dust attacked seedlings with ICI Sybol 2 Dust, or spray with Murphy Fentro, or pbi Fenitrothion.

Chocolate Spot *Leaves blotched with brownish spots. Plant may turn black and die.* CURE: Avoid growing in soils too rich in nitrogen. Burn all crop debris at the end of the season to destroy fungal spores. Spray with pbi Benlate, ICI General Garden Fungicide, or Synchemicals' Bordeaux Mixture.

Rust *Raised orange spots underneath the leaves.* CURE: Only severe outbreaks need to be sprayed with Murphy Liquid Copper Fungicide or ICI General Garden Fungicide.

Seeds failing to emerge after sowing may have fallen prey to fungal diseases. CURE: Sow in well-drained soil which is not too cold. Treat seeds before sowing with Murphy Combined Seed Dressing.

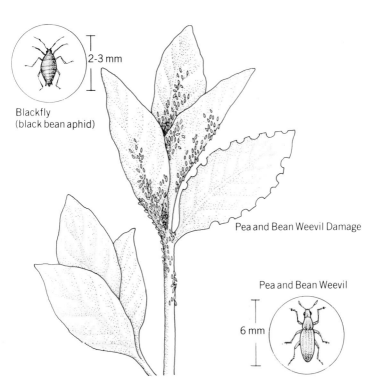

2-3 mm

Blackfly
(black bean aphid)

Pea and Bean Weevil Damage

Pea and Bean Weevil

6 mm

FRENCH AND RUNNER BEAN

Both crops require excellent drainage, a fertile soil and plenty of sun and water during the growing season.

PROBLEMS

Red Spider Mite *Leaves turn greyish or yellow. Fine webs observed and pin-prick-sized green mites seen on undersides of leaves.* CURE: Discourage attacks by spraying foliage daily with water. Spray infestations with Bio Systemic Insecticide, Murphy Systemic Insecticide, or Murphy Liquid Malathion three times at the interval recommended on the label.

Anthracnose *Leaves and stems blotched with brown. Sunken brown blotches on pods, often edged with red.* CURE: Burn all infected plants. Buy seeds from a reputable source (they can carry this fungus disease). Destroy crop debris at end of season. Dust seeds with pbi Benlate before sowing. Spray with pbi Benlate at fortnightly intervals until flowers open.

Halo Blight *Brown blotches edged with yellow found on leaves. Soggy spots appear later on pods.* CURE: Buy seeds from a reputable source. Burn infected plants at end of season.

Flower Drop *Flowers drop off and no pods are produced.* CURE: Water regularly. Net crops to keep out birds. Spray open flowers with water to assist pollination. Grow crops in groups on tripods rather than in long rows.

Foot Rot *Stem bases turn black and rot. Leaves yellow.* CURE: Crop rotation. Water seedlings with Cheshunt Compound.

Halo Blight

Anthracnose

BEETROOT
Grow on well-worked and well-drained soil that is not too rich in manure. In over-rich stony ground the roots may become forked or distorted. Rapid fluctuation in moisture content may lead to bolting.

PROBLEMS

Blackfly *Masses of small black insects on leaves.* CURE: Spray with ICI Rapid Greenfly Killer, Boots Greenfly Killer, or Murphy Liquid Malathion.

Beet Leaf Miner *Yellow or brown tunnels or blisters on leaves. Grubs found inside.* CURE: Squeeze leaf between finger and thumb to crush grubs. Pick off badly infected leaves and spray plants with May & Baker Caterpillar Killer, Bio Systemic Insecticide, or Murphy Systemic Insecticide.

Bolting *Plants send up tall flower stem instead of normal leaf cluster.* CURE: Grow varieties resistant to bolting (e.g. Boltardy). Do not sow too early. Do not allow crop to go short of moisture. Thin seedlings before they compete with one another.

Downy Mildew *Leaves yellowish; mouldy on undersides.* CURE: Pick off infected leaves and destroy them. Spray with ICI General Garden Fungicide, Murphy Liquid Copper Fungicide, Synchemicals' Bordeaux Mixture, or pbi Dithane 945. Space plants adequately to avoid attack.

For **Slug** control see page 52.

Downy Mildew

CABBAGE, CAULIFLOWER, BROCCOLI AND BRUSSELS SPROUTS

Known collectively as 'brassicas', these crops need a firm, fertile soil that is well-drained but not subject to drought.

PROBLEMS

Mealy Cabbage Aphid *Leaves turn yellow. Colonies of small grey insects found on undersides.* CURE: Prevent attack by destroying crop debris at end of season. Spray outbreaks with Murphy Fentro, pbi Fenitrothion, or pbi Crop Saver.

Cabbage Caterpillar *Leaves eaten. Caterpillars found.* CURE: Pick off caterpillars by hand if infestation is small. Spray larger outbreaks with ICI Picket, Bio Flydown, or May & Baker Caterpillar Killer.

Cabbage Root Fly *Leaves turn blue-grey; plants wilt and are stunted. Roots eaten away by white maggots.* CURE: Treat the soil around young plants with Murphy Soil Pest Killer, Fison's Combat Soil Insecticide, or May & Baker Soil Insecticide Granules. Water established plants with May & Baker Caterpillar Killer. Bituminised paper rings round young plants discourage egg-laying flies.

Gall Weevil *Plants stunted. Roots swollen and grubs or holes observed when swellings cut open.* CURE: Attacks are seldom fatal. Grow plants in good soil. Dust around young plants with pbi Bromophos, ICI Sybol 2 Dust, or Murphy Soil Pest Killer at planting time.

Cabbage Whitefly *Tiny, white, 'V'-shaped flies on undersides of leaves.* CURE: Spray severe outbreaks with ICI Picket, Bio Flydown, or ICI Sybol 2 at the recommended intervals.

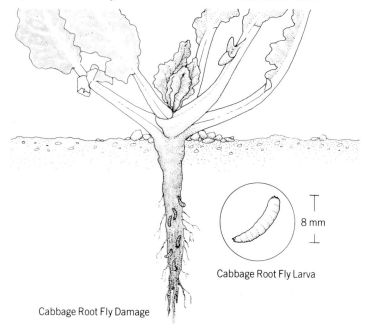

8 mm

Cabbage Root Fly Larva

Cabbage Root Fly Damage

Pigeons *Leaves torn and shredded. No insects visible.*
CURE: Cover crops.
No hearts formed. CURE: Make sure soil contains sufficient organic matter, is firm, and is not allowed to dry out.
Clubroot *Plants stunted and wilting. Roots found to be swollen and foul-smelling. No holes present.* CURE: Practise crop rotation. Lime acid soils before planting. Make sure drainage is good. Dip roots of young plants in Murphy Systemic Clubroot Dip. pbi Benlate, or any fungicide containing calomel.
Grey Mould *Leaves grey and mouldy or brown and rotten.* CURE: Pick off and destroy infected leaves. Prevent the fungus attacking by applying 14 g (½ oz) sulphate of potash to 0.83 m² (1 sq yd) of ground before planting.

Clubroot (finger and toe disease)

Powdery Mildew *White, powdery deposit on upper surface of leaves.* CURE: Spray severe attacks with pbi Benlate. Space plants well.
Downy Mildew *Leaves yellow above; white and fluffy below.* CURE: Space plants sufficiently to avoid attack. Spray affected plants with pbi Dithane 945, ICI General Garden Fungicide, or Bordeaux Mixture.
Whiptail *Leaves reduced to a thin midrib but no pest damage observed.* CURE: Dilute 28 g (1 oz) sodium molybdate in 9 litres (2 galls) water and apply to each 8.3 m² (10 sq yd) of soil. Lime acid soil.

For **Slug** control see page 52.

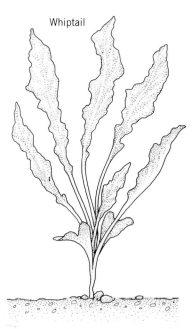

Whiptail

CARROT AND PARSNIP

Both these root crops enjoy a well-cultivated and well-drained soil which has been kept free of stones and is not too rich in manure.

PROBLEMS

Carrot Fly *Leaves turn reddish and wilt in bright sunshine; roots are tunnelled by small creamy-white grubs.* CURE: Avoid by sowing thinly and by not thinning out the seedlings. Late May sowings can often escape attack. Scatter Murphy Soil Pest Killer, Fison's Combat Soil Insecticide, or May & Baker Soil Insecticide Granules along the seed drill at sowing time.

Parsnip Canker *Upper areas of parsnip roots turn brown and rot.* CURE: Prevent by ensuring that the crop is not over-manured. Avoid sowing on acid soils and do not sow too early. Sow resistant varieties (e.g. Avonresister; Tender & True). Practise crop rotation.

Fanging *Roots forked.* CURE: Prevent by growing crop in well-cultivated soil which is free of stones and which has not been freshly manured.

Soft Rot *Carrots go soft and rotten in ground or in store.* CURE: Avoid heavy manuring and waterlogged soil. Store only undamaged roots.

Splitting *Roots split longitudinally.* CURE: Avoid by ensuring that the soil is kept moist at all times. Splitting is most commonly caused by sudden rain or other applications of water after drought.

Violet Root Rot *Roots of carrots possess purple felted patches.* CURE: Destroy all infected roots. Practise crop rotation. Do not grow carrots in soil infected with this fungus for at least four or five years.

For **Aphid** control see page 52.

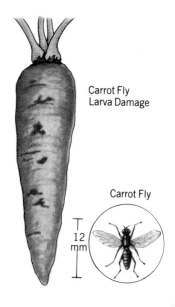

Carrot Fly
Larva Damage

Carrot Fly

12
mm

PEA, GARDEN

Like beans, garden peas need a rich, moisture-retentive soil and plenty of sun. The ground should be dug deeply a few months before sowing. Harvest the pods as soon as they are ripe, otherwise the size of the crop will be reduced.

PROBLEMS

Pea Moth *Peas found to be maggoty when pods opened.* CURE: Prevent by spraying with Murphy Fentro, or pbi Fenitrothion, one week after the flowers have opened. Spray in the evening when bees are not active.

Pea Thrips *Pods spotted and blotched with silver-grey.* CURE: Spray at first signs of damage with Murphy Fentro, or pbi Fenitrothion.

Pea & Bean Weevil *The edges of the leaves are scalloped.* CURE: See page 53.

Foot Rot *The stem bases turn black and then rot. Leaves turn yellow.* CURE: See page 54.

Grey Mould *Pods mouldy and rotten.* CURE: Pick off and destroy badly infected pods. Spray plants with pbi Benlate, or Murphy Systemic Fungicide. Ensure good air circulation around the plants.

Downy Mildew *Leaves yellow on upper surface, purplish below. Pods distorted.* CURE: Spray with pbi Dithane 945 at fortnightly intervals. Destroy badly infected plants. Practise crop rotation.

Powdery Mildew *Leaves covered in white powder. Pods affected too.* CURE: Spray at fortnightly intervals with pbi Benlate. Ensure good air circulation. Sow resistant varieties such as Kelvedon Wonder.

Virus Disease *Leaves mottled with yellow; pods are rough; plants stunted.* CURE: Prevent by controlling aphids. Destroy all infected plants.

For **Aphid** and **Bird** control see page 52.

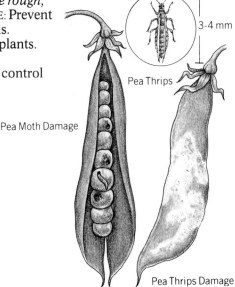

3-4 mm

Pea Thrips

Pea Moth Damage

Pea Thrips Damage

POTATO
Grow potatoes on well-drained, well-manured soil in good light.

PROBLEMS

Potato Cyst Eelworm *Lower leaves turn brown and shrivel. Plants stunted and pale, dying down prematurely. Tiny nodules or 'cysts' on roots. Potatoes small and few in number.* CURE: Destroy all infected plants, including tubers. Do not grow potatoes or tomatoes in infected soil for at least eight years. Grow resistant varieties such as Pentland Javelin and Maris Piper. Practise crop rotation.

Slugs *Tubers found to be riddled with holes or even hollow when harvested. Small black slugs present.* CURE: Prevent damage by lifting tubers as soon as possible or by growing early varieties which are less frequently decimated. Where slugs are a problem, avoid heavy applications of manure or organic fertilisers. Lay slug pellets or traps around the plants in warm, humid weather. Do not store damaged tubers.

Wireworms *Narrow tunnels made in tubers. Usually a problem on newly cultivated land.* CURE: Harvest tubers as soon as possible. Rake pbi Bromophos, Murphy Soil Pest Killer, or Fison's Combat Soil Insecticide into the soil at planting time.

Virus Disease *Leaves curled inwards, or leaves mottled with yellow.* CURE: Prevent by planting certified seed potatoes and by keeping down aphids. Destroy infected plants and tubers. Check that plants have not been affected by frost which can also cause yellowing but which is not fatal.

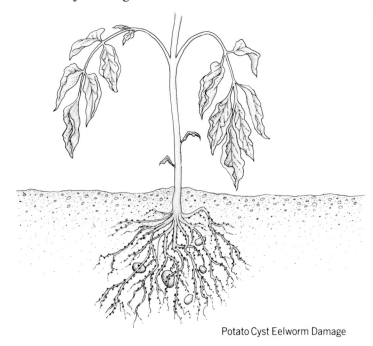

Potato Cyst Eelworm Damage

Potato Blight *Leaves are blotched with brown and tend to curl inwards. White mould present on undersides of leaves. Later in the season tubers may show red-brown areas.* CURE: Plant certified seed potatoes. Spray with Bordeaux Mixture, or pbi Dithane 945 at fortnightly intervals from July onwards, or earlier if attacks are noticed. Plant potatoes 15 cm (6 in) deep and earth up generously to prevent tubers from being infected by falling fungal spores. Grow resistant varieties such as Maris Peer, Pentland Crown, Stormont Enterprise.

Frost Damage *Leaves suddenly turn yellow, brown or black.* CURE: Prevent by not planting too early. Earth up young shoots regularly. Epicure is more resistant to damage than most early varieties.

Gangrene *Sunken brown areas on tubers in store. Flesh rotten.* CURE: Store only healthy, undamaged tubers in airy, frost-free conditions.

Scab *Tubers covered in rough brown scabs.* CURE: Prevent by avoiding the use of lime. Grow resistant varieties such as Arran Pilot, Maris Peer, Pentland Crown, Pentland Javelin. Potatoes are still edible if attacked.

Powdery Scab *Dark brown, circular scabs with raised edges found on tubers.* CURE: Prevent by growing potatoes in well-drained soil. Destroy infected tubers. Practise crop rotation. Pentland Crown is very susceptible to this disease.

Spraing *Tubers found to be marked with red semi-circles when cut open.* CURE: Prevent this virus disease by practising

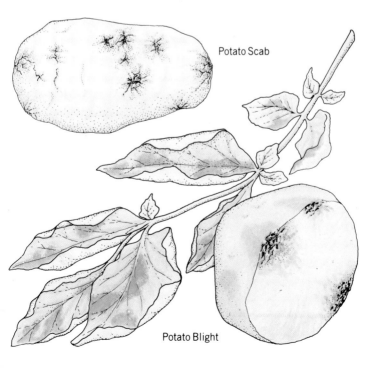

Potato Scab

Potato Blight

crop rotation. Avoid growing Pentland Dell which is very susceptible. Plant certified seed potatoes. Tubers are edible but should not be saved for seed.

Blackleg *Stem bases blackened; leaves turn yellow and wilt.* CURE: Dig up and destroy any plants with this fungus infection. Store only healthy tubers that show no signs of rot, and lift the entire crop as soon as the disease is noticed.

Dry Rot *Tubers in store wrinkle at one end, and white or pink fungal growth is observed.* CURE: Prevent by lifting with care and storing tubers in a well-ventilated place. Destroy any infected tubers.

Green Tubers *Tubers green and unpleasant tasting.* CURE: Earth up properly to prevent the tubers from being exposed to the sun. Do not eat green tubers.

Hollow Heart *Tubers found to be hollow when cut open, but no evidence of slug or wireworm damage.* CURE: Keep soil evenly moist at all times. Caused by sudden and usually prolonged application of water after drought. Tubers may eventually rot.

Wart Disease *Black, wart-like growths appear on the tubers of old varieties. Tubers become distorted and rotten.* CURE: Burn all infected tubers. The Ministry of Agriculture should be informed of outbreaks of this fungus disease. Grow new potato varieties which are all immune to attack e.g. Maris Piper, Pentland Javelin.

For **Aphid** control see page 52.

Blackleg

RADISH In a rich soil with plenty of moisture, radishes will grow so fast that pests and diseases have little time to strike.

PROBLEM
Flea Beetle *Tiny spots and holes in leaves.* CURE: Dust the plants with Derris at the first sign of attack. Keep the crop growing well so that attacks can be shrugged off.

RHUBARB To grow really well rhubarb needs plenty of light and a rich, moisture-retentive soil.

PROBLEMS
Crown Rot *Buds and centre of plant brown and rotten.* CURE: Dig up and burn infected plants. Make sure that soil is well drained before planting. Do not replant rhubarb on ground where this bacterial disease has occurred.
Honey Fungus *Plants die. White fungus found in roots and crown. Black 'bootlaces' found in soil in some cases.* CURE: Dig up and burn infected plants. Plant rhubarb on a site that has not been previously occupied by trees and shrubs. Do not replant rhubarb in infected soil.
Leaf Spot *Brown spots on leaves. Centres fall out leaving holes.* CURE: Remove and burn infected leaves. Not severe. Make sure the plant has an adequate food supply.

For **Aphid** control see page 52.

3-4 mm

Flea Beetle

Flea Beetle Damage

Rhubarb Crown Rot

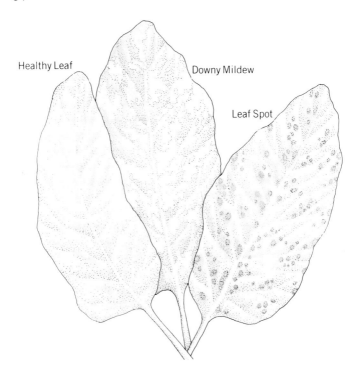

Healthy Leaf · Downy Mildew · Leaf Spot

SPINACH
A crop that does well in an enriched soil. Grow spinach in sun or light shade.

PROBLEMS
Spinach Blight *Leaves roll inwards and become yellowish.*
CURE: This is a virus disease so all infected plants should be pulled up and burned. Control aphids by spraying with ICI Rapid Greenfly Killer – these insects carry the disease. Keep down weeds which may also harbour aphids.

Bolting *Plants form flower stalks prematurely.* CURE: Prevent by making sure the plants *never* go short of water and that the soil is moisture retentive. Most troublesome in dry summers. Starved plants may also bolt.

Leaf Spot *Leaves spotted with brown or purple; centres of spots usually fall out.* CURE: Remove infected leaves. Practise crop rotation. Avoid applying too much nitrogenous fertiliser. Space plants adequately.

Downy Mildew *Leaves with yellow areas on upper surface, purplish below. Affected areas eventually turn brown.* CURE: Remove and destroy leaves showing signs of attack. Spray plants with pbi Dithane 945. Avoid applying too much high nitrogen fertiliser as this will encourage sappy growth that is very susceptible to the fungus. Ensure that plants are spaced adequately.

SWEDE AND TURNIP
A well-cultivated soil manured for a previous crop will suit both these root vegetables.

PROBLEMS
Cabbage Root Fly *Roots eaten and tunnelled; small white maggots observed.* CURE: See page 56.

Flea Beetle *Leaves covered in tiny spots and holes.* CURE: See page 63.

Gall Weevil *Roots possess spherical swellings which, when cut open, are found to contain maggots or tunnels.* CURE: See page 56.

Black Rot *Leaves yellow at edges with black veins. Roots found to be black around the edge when cut open.* CURE: Pull up and burn diseased plants. Prevent by growing crop on well-drained soil. A bacterial disease. Practise crop rotation.

Brown Heart *Brown discoloration noticed in roots when they are sliced open. Stringy and unpleasant when cooked.* CURE: Due to boron deficiency, so apply a balanced fertiliser before sowing, or borax at the rate of 28 g (1 oz) to 16.72 m² (20 sq yd) if the deficiency has previously been a problem. Mix the borax with sand to make even application easier.

Clubroot *Roots swollen and foul smelling. No holes present.* CURE: See page 57.

Powdery Mildew *Leaves covered in white powder.* CURE: See page 57.

Soft Rot *Leaves collapse; top and inside of root brown and rotten.* CURE: Pull up and destroy plants infected with this bacterium, and any rotten stored roots. Practise crop rotation. Ensure good drainage and avoid over-manuring and mechanical damage to roots.

Virus Disease *Leaves badly distorted or mottled with yellow.* CURE: Pull up and burn infected plants. Control aphids which spread the disease – spray with ICI Rapid Greenfly Killer as soon as attacks are seen.

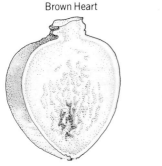

Brown Heart

Black Rot

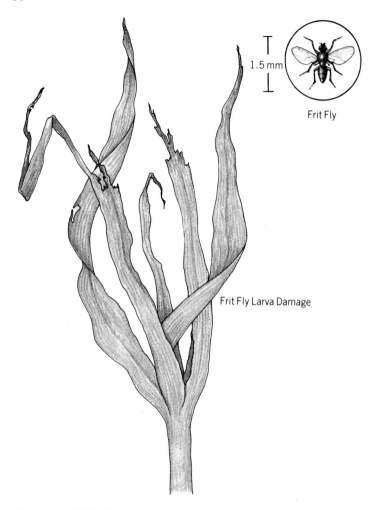

1.5 mm

Frit Fly

Frit Fly Larva Damage

SWEET CORN Best grown in a well-cultivated and
moderately rich soil in a sunny, sheltered spot.

PROBLEMS

Frit Fly *Young plants twisted and distorted, leaves ragged.*
CURE: Raise plants in greenhouse and plant out when growing
strongly to discourage attack. Keep plants growing well, and
dust with Murphy Gamma-BHC Dust as a preventive measure.
Smut *Large, white, inflated outgrowths on cobs and stems;
black spores revealed if outgrowths burst open.* CURE: Cut out
and burn all 'galls' before they burst and scatter their
spores. Burn all plants when the cobs have been harvested. Do
not grow sweet corn in ground which is infected with this
fungus for at least three years. This disease is particularly
common in very long, hot summers.
Cobs with many undeveloped kernels. CURE: Plant in blocks
rather than rows to ensure good pollination.

HEALTHY FRUIT

Pests and diseases on bush fruits and strawberries are comparatively easy to control, but large trees are rather more difficult to cover with a sprayer. Get round this problem by growing dwarf forms of tree, or reconcile yourself to the fact that some harmful organisms will go unchecked. The following pests and diseases are likely to attack a wide range of fruit crops:

Aphids Greenfly, blackfly and their relatives look unsightly and they weaken the plant. Aphids spread virus diseases and secrete honeydew that is colonised by a black fungus called sooty mould. Spray fruit trees in winter to kill off overwintering eggs. Use Murphy Mortegg, or ICI Clean Up. Summer infestations on other fruits can be controlled by spraying with ICI Rapid Greenfly Killer, or Abol-G.

Birds More difficult to keep in check on fruits than on vegetables, which are usually a more manageable size. See page 52 for control measures, and remember that they will be needed from the moment the leaves fall in autumn until after the flower petals fall in spring (as far as tree fruit blossom protection is concerned). Soft fruits may be susceptible only as the fruits ripen.

Rabbits and deer Both these animals can be discouraged by spraying trees and crops with Scoot. Stay-Off Spiral rabbit guards made of flexible plastic are the best long-term protection for young trees.

Honey fungus See page 84 for details of recognition and control.

Stem-boring caterpillars The sudden die-back of one isolated stem on a fruit tree or bush may be due to the presence of a stem-boring caterpillar at the core of the shoot. Cut out the affected stem and destroy the larva.

Rabbit Guard Around Young Tree

APPLE A long-term crop for good, deep, well-drained soil and a sheltered sunny position.

PROBLEMS

Aphids *Leaves are covered in greenfly or blackfly.* CURE: See page 67.

Capsid Bug *Leaves perforated with small holes; fruits possess raised brown areas like smooth scabs.* CURE: Spray when the flower buds are visible (but not open) with Murphy Fentro or pbi Fenitrothion. If the pest has been a great problem in previous years, give a second spray after the petals have fallen.

Codling Moth *Fruits found to be maggoty when harvested.* CURE: Spray twice with Murphy Fentro or pbi Fenitrothion; first in mid-June, then again in mid-July.

Apple Sawfly *Fruitlets fall and are found to be tunnelled; some remaining on tree have a long, brown scar.* CURE: Pick off infected fruits if tree is small. Spray with Murphy Fentro, or pbi Fenitrothion when most of the flower petals have fallen.

Red Spider Mite *Leaves bleached and mottled; tiny greenish-yellow mites visible on undersides.* CURE: Spray in February with Murphy Mortegg or ICI Clean Up as a winter wash to kill overwintering eggs. Spray with Bio Systemic Insecticide, Murphy Systemic Insecticide, or Boots Greenfly Killer in summer.

Apple Sucker *Flowers turn brown; tiny, green, aphid-like insects are found on them.* CURE: Use ICI Clean Up or Murphy Mortegg winter washes in February to kill overwintering eggs. Apply one of the systemic insecticides previously mentioned when the closed flower buds are visible.

Tortrix Moth *Surface of fruit eaten and a leaf stuck over the damaged area. Caterpillar may be observed.* CURE: Use one of the winter washes previously mentioned to kill overwintering eggs. Spray with Murphy Fentro or pbi Fenitrothion when the fruitlets have formed.

Winter Moth *Open flowers and young leaves eaten; small green caterpillars may be observed.* CURE: Fasten Boltac Greasebands around the trunks of the trees from September to March to prevent the adult moths from scaling the tree and laying eggs. Spray outbreaks in spring with Murphy Fentro or pbi Fenitrothion.

Woolly Aphid *Stems colonised by small insects covered in white wool.* CURE: Spray as soon as seen with Boots Systemic Greenfly Killer, Murphy Systemic Insecticide, or Bio Systemic Insecticide. Paint the diluted solution on to bad infestations.

Apple Scab *Fruits covered in rough, dark brown scabs.* CURE: Spray with pbi Benlate at fortnightly intervals from the time the shoots burst open until midsummer.

Bitter Pit *Fruits covered in dark brown spots which go through to the flesh. Often appears on fruit in store.* CURE: Never allow the tree to go short of water during the growing season. If the disorder is a persistent problem, spray the tree with calcium nitrate diluted in water at the rate of 28 g (1 oz) in 9 litres (2 galls) in mid-June. Repeat several times at fortnightly intervals.

Blossom Wilt *Flowers wilt and turn brown; leaves may die back. Most commonly troublesome in wet springs.* CURE: Cut off all infected shoots as soon as they are seen. Spray with pbi Benlate just before the flowers open to discourage the disease.

Brown Rot *Fruits go brown and rotten on tree or in store. Concentric circles of grey, green or buff pustules appear.* CURE: Prevent mechanical and insect damage to fruits. Store only sound fruits in a clean, airy store.

Apple Canker *Stems found to be wounded and, in winter, the wounds possess small red fruiting bodies.* CURE: Cut out all infected branches and paint cut surfaces with May & Baker Seal & Heal Pruning Paint. Keep trees well supplied with water and nutrients. Control woolly aphids which allow disease to enter.

Fireblight *Shoots wither and turn brown but the leaves do not fall. Wound-like 'cankers' can be observed at the base of infected shoots in autumn and spring. Tree looks burned.* CURE: The local office of the Ministry of Agriculture should be informed if you suspect that your tree has this bacterial disease. Mild cases can be controlled by pruning the infected stems well back into healthy tissue which is not stained brown. Apply May & Baker Seal & Heal Pruning Paint to cut surfaces.

Fruit Drop *Fruitlets fall before fully developed.* CURE: If no maggots are present (see **Sawfly**, page 68) then soil conditions may be at fault (make sure moisture and nutrients are present in sufficient quantity), or the flowers may not have been successfully fertilised (in which case pollen from another apple tree may be needed to ensure a crop in future years). A fair number of fruitlets drop naturally in June (known as June drop) and should not give cause for alarm.

Honey Fungus *Tree suffering from severe die-back. Black bootlace-like structures found in soil, or white fungal growth under bark at ground level.* CURE: See page 84.

Powdery Mildew *Leaves and shoots covered in white powder.* CURE: Spray with pbi Benlate or Murphy Systemic Fungicide fortnightly from the time you can see the closed green flower buds, until late summer. Prune out affected shoots in winter.

Lack of fruits may be caused by blossoms being frosted, or the lack of pollen for pollination (see **Fruit Drop** above).

APRICOT, ALMOND, PEACH AND NECTARINE

These fruits produce their best crops in well-drained soil that is not too acid. All need sun and shelter.

PROBLEMS

Red Spider Mite *Leaves become dull and bleached grey-green or yellow. Minute mites visible on undersides.* CURE: Spray in December with ICI Clean Up, or Murphy Mortegg. Spray summer outbreaks with Bio Systemic Insecticide, Boots Systemic Greenfly Killer, or Murphy Systemic Insecticide.

Brown Scale *Stems covered with small brown scales.* CURE: Spray in December with ICI Clean Up, or Murphy Mortegg. Spray in July with Murphy Liquid Malathion, Boots Greenfly Killer, or pbi Malathion Greenfly Killer.

Peach Leaf Curl *Leaves curled and puckered with large red blisters, eventually turning whitish.* CURE: Prevent the fungus from attacking by spraying the shoots before the buds open in January with Synchemicals' Bordeaux Mixture, or Murphy Liquid Copper Fungicide. Spray again a fortnight later and repeat just before the leaves start to fall in autumn. Pick off and burn badly infected leaves. Gather and burn fallen leaves in autumn.

Shothole *Leaves develop brown spots which eventually fall away to leave small holes.* CURE: Prevent this fungus from attacking by making sure that trees have ample supplies of food and water. Spray with foliar feed at first sign of attack, and with Murphy Liquid Copper Fungicide diluted to half its recommended strength if the disease gets out of hand.

Powdery Mildew *Leaves covered in white powder, but no blistering or reddening noticeable. Young leaves may fall.* CURE: Spray with pbi Toprose Mildew Spray, or dust with Synchemicals' Green and Yellow Sulphur.

For **Aphid** control see page 67.

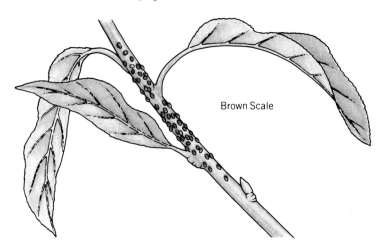

Brown Scale

BLACKBERRY AND LOGANBERRY

Both these fruits are tolerant of a wide range of soils, and both crops will grow in full sun or light shade.

PROBLEMS

Raspberry Beetle *Fruits maggoty or eaten.* CURE: Prevent attack by spraying blackberries with pbi Liquid Derris, or Murphy Derris Liquid just as the flowers open. Spray in the evening when bees are not active. Loganberries will need two sprays – one when most of the petals have fallen and another a fortnight later.

Crown Gall *Lumpy galls present on stems at ground level or higher up.* CURE: Cut out and burn all infected stems. Any plants badly infected with this bacterial disease should be burnt. Plant healthy new stock on a different patch of ground. Prevent attacks by ensuring good drainage, and avoiding mechanical damage.

Spur Blight *Areas of loganberry stems around buds turn purplish in late summer; later they become silver and the portion of the stem dies. Buds fail to produce shoots in spring, or the shoots quickly wilt and die.* CURE: See under Raspberry, page 81.

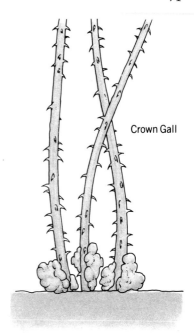

Crown Gall

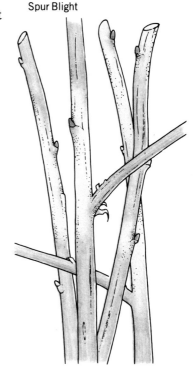

Spur Blight

For **Aphid** control see page 67.

CHERRY Sweet cherries may prove too large for the average-sized garden, but the morello cherry (good for cooking and preserving) will do well against a north-facing wall. It enjoys well-drained soil which is not too acid, so most soils will need liming before a cherry tree is planted.

PROBLEMS

Cherry Blackfly *Leaves curled under at the edges and infested with masses of small black insects; shoots stunted and weakened.* CURE: Prevent by spraying the newly opened shoots with ICI Rapid Greenfly Killer, or Abol-G. Repeat when the petals have fallen from the flowers and whenever an attack is noticed. Spraying the trees in February with ICI Clean Up, or Murphy Mortegg, will kill overwintering eggs.

Cherry Fruit Moth *Small green caterpillars feeding in buds and on open flowers; fruits found to be maggoty while still green.* CURE: Spray trees with a winter wash such as Murphy Mortegg, or ICI Clean Up, in February to kill overwintering eggs.

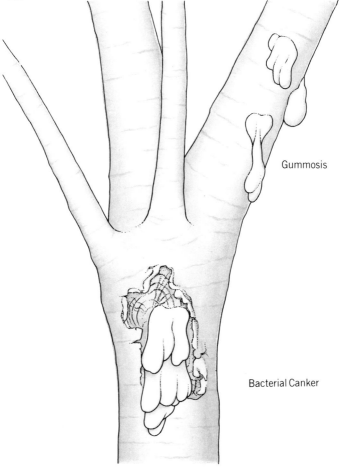

Gummosis

Bacterial Canker

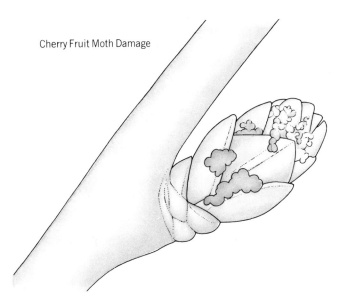

Cherry Fruit Moth Damage

Gummosis *Gummy substance oozing from otherwise healthy bark.* CURE: Caused by lack of water or nutrients. Feed tree with general fertiliser at 112 g (4 oz) to 0.83 m² (1 sq yd). Ensure water supplies are adequate. Cut off hardened gum with a sharp knife and paint wound with May & Baker Seal & Heal Pruning Paint.

Bacterial Canker *Flattened cankers appear on trunk and branches, gum oozes from them; branches lose vigour and may die. The leaves are full of holes.* CURE: Cut out and burn all infected branches, making cuts well back into healthy tissue. Paint cut surfaces with May & Baker Seal & Heal Pruning Paint. Spray trees with a proprietary Bordeaux Mixture once a month from August to October (three applications in all).

Shothole *Leaves full of small holes; brown spots also present.* CURE: Make sure that tree is well fed (a foliar feed will boost it quickly) and not short of water. If gum oozes from the bark suspect **Bacterial Canker** (see above).

Silver Leaf *Leaves on one particular branch (or a few branches) look silvery. When the stem is cut through the wood is found to be stained brown. Shoots may also die back.* CURE: Cut out all infected branches at least 15 cm (6 in) past the point at which internal staining stops. Sterilise pruning tools afterwards, and paint cuts with May & Baker Seal & Heal Pruning Paint. Burn all infected wood. If purplish bracket fungi appear on the trunk then fell and burn the tree.

False Silver Leaf *Leaves all over the tree turn silvery. No pronounced die-back of stem tips.* CURE: Make sure the tree is not short of water. Spray with a foliar feed. This disorder is caused by starvation and lack of moisture in the soil.

For **Bird** control see page 67.

CURRANT
All currants like a good, well-drained soil. Black currants will tolerate a little shade.

PROBLEMS
Capsid Bug *Leaves punctured with small holes that have brown edges; some puckering noticeable.* CURE: Spray with Bio Systemic Insecticide, Boots Systemic Greenfly Killer, or Murphy Systemic Insecticide once the petals have fallen from the flowers.

Big Bud Mite (Black Currant Gall Mite) *Buds on dormant black currant stems fat and swollen.* CURE: Prune out and burn infected shoots as soon as they are noticed in winter. The fungicide pbi Benlate can discourage attacks if it is sprayed on to the plants when the flowers start to open. Spray twice more at fortnightly intervals. Dig up and burn badly infected bushes and replant healthy ones on fresh ground. Big bud mite carries **Reversion Disease.**

Leaf Midge *Shoot tips distorted and withered.* CURE: Spray with Bio Systemic Insecticide, Boots Systemic Greenfly Killer, or Murphy Systemic Insecticide just before the flowers open.

Sawfly *Leaves badly eaten; in some cases only the veins are left; caterpillars visible.* CURE: Spray with Murphy Fentro, or pbi Fenitrothion as soon as damage noticed. If fruits are near maturity spray instead with Derris.

Reversion Disease *Foliage distorted; leaves have fewer lobes; flowers pinkish-purple instead of pale green.* CURE: None. This

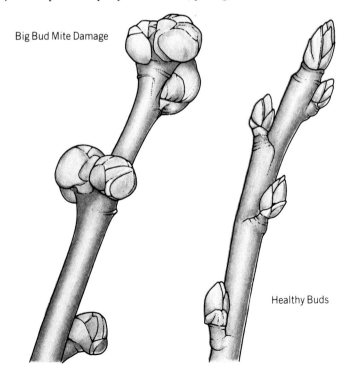

Big Bud Mite Damage

Healthy Buds

disease causes a drastic reduction in cropping. Burn infected bushes. Plant clean stock on a new site. Control **Big Bud Mite.**

Coral Spot *Stems dying back and showing raised orange spots.* CURE: Cut out all dead or infected wood and paint wounds with May & Baker Seal & Heal Pruning Paint. Prevent by pruning with sharp secateurs in the first place. Sterilise the pruning tools after use.

Leaf Spot *Leaves develop small brown spots which join together to form larger areas; leaves eventually fall.* CURE: Gather and burn all fallen leaves in autumn. Spray bushes with pbi Benlate once before the flowers open and three times more at fortnightly intervals.

American Gooseberry Mildew *Shoots and leaves covered with white powder which eventually becomes felt-like and turns light brown. The fruits are also affected.* CURE: Prevent by pruning to ensure good air circulation through bushes; avoid applying high nitrogen fertilisers which encourage sappy growth. Cut out and burn badly infected shoots. Spray bushes with pbi Benlate once before the flowers open and three times more at fortnightly intervals.

Botrytis *Fruits covered in grey mould.* CURE: Prevent by spraying with Murphy Systemic Fungicide, or pbi Benlate, when the flowers open and three times more at fortnightly intervals.

For **Aphid** control see page 67.

Leaf Spot

Reversion

PEAR Pears, like apples, need a deep, fertile, well-drained soil and a site that is not in a frost pocket.

PROBLEMS

Codling Moth *Fruits found to be maggoty when harvested.* CURE: See page 68.

Pear Leaf Blister Mite *Pale green or pink spots appear on the leaves at either side of the main central vein. Eventually the spots turn dark brown or black.* CURE: Pick off and burn badly infected leaves if this is practicable. Make sure that the tree is well supplied with water and nutrients so that it can shrug off attacks. No chemical treatment necessary.

Pear Midge *Fruitlets turn brown and fall from tree when quite small; if cut open many yellowish maggots are found inside, or fruit will be eaten and hollow.* CURE: Remove and burn infested fruitlets. Prevent attack by spraying trees with Murphy Fentro, or pbi Fenitrothion before the flowers open but when the buds are white.

Pear Sawfly *Fruitlets fall and are found to be tunnelled by a single maggot. Mature fruits on tree may show a ribbon-shaped scar.* CURE: See **Apple Sawfly**, page 68.

Pear Sucker *Flowers and young leaves turn brown and tiny green insects can be found sucking sap.* CURE: See **Apple Sucker**, page 68.

Red Spider Mite or **Bryobia Mite** *Leaves bleached grey-green or yellow; tiny yellow, green or rusty coloured mites observed on undersides.* CURE: See page 68.

Pear Leaf Blister Mite Damage

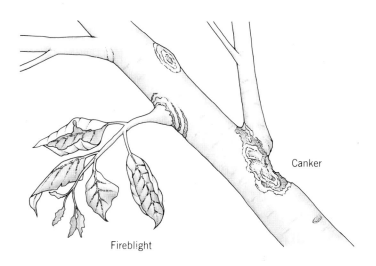

Canker

Fireblight

Slugworm *Small, black, slug-like creatures on leaves.* CURE: Not usually worth bothering about. Severe infestations can be controlled by spraying with Derris.

Winter Moth *Flowers and new leaves eaten; green caterpillars noticed.* CURE: See page 68.

Blossom Wilt *Flowers wilt and turn brown; leaves may die back.* CURE: See page 69.

Canker *Stems wounded, and in winter the wounds carry small, red fruiting bodies.* CURE: See **Apple Canker**, page 69.

Honey Fungus *Tree suffering from severe die-back. Black bootlace-like growths found in surrounding soil, or white fungal growth found beneath bark at soil level.* CURE: See page 84.

Fireblight *Shoots wither and turn brown but the leaves do not fall. Wound like 'cankers' can be observed at the base of infected shoots in autumn and spring. Tree looks burned.* CURE: See page 69.

Pear Scab *Fruits covered in rough, dark brown scabs.* CURE: See **Apple Scab,** page 69.

For **Aphid** control see page 67.

PLUM
Plums make large trees and enjoy a sunny, sheltered site and a deep soil that is not too acid.

PROBLEMS

Mussel Scale *Small mussel-shaped scales closely packed on stems.* CURE: Spray with Murphy Mortegg, or ICI Clean Up in January. Summer infestations can be sprayed with Murphy Liquid Malathion, Boots Greenfly Killer, or pbi Malathion Greenfly Killer.

Plum Sawfly *Fruitlets fall before they are fully developed; when cut open a tunnel is visible.* CURE: Spray with Murphy Fentro, or pbi Fenitrothion one week after all the petals have fallen to prevent attack.

Red Spider Mite *Leaves bleached grey-green or yellow; minute yellow or green mites visible on undersides.* CURE: See page 68.

Plum Tortrix Moth *Leaves wrapped together with fine silken threads and caterpillars found to be feeding inside.* CURE: Spray trees in January with ICI Clean Up, or Murphy Mortegg. Spray in April with Murphy Fentro, or pbi Fenitrothion.

Wasp *Ripening fruit eaten by wasps.* CURE: Seek out and destroy nests if this is thought to be necessary. Wall-trained trees can be hung with old net curtains or muslin to keep out wasps during the fruit ripening period.

Winter Moth *Flowers and young leaves eaten; green caterpillars observed.* CURE: See page 68.

Bacterial Canker *Flattened cankers appear on branches and gum oozes from them; branches lose vigour and may die. Leaves full of holes.* CURE: See page 73.

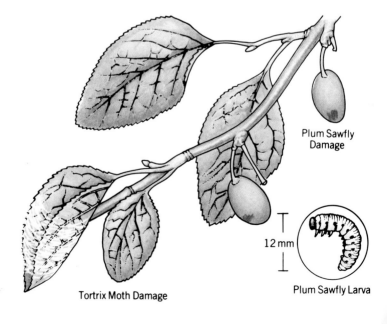

Plum Sawfly Damage

Tortrix Moth Damage

12 mm

Plum Sawfly Larva

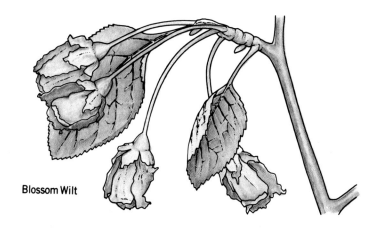

Blossom Wilt

Blossom Wilt *Flowers wilt and turn brown; leaves may die back.* CURE: See page 69.

Brown Rot *Fruits go brown and rotten; concentric circles of grey, green or buff pustules appear.* CURE: See page 69.

Plum Rust *Leaves spotted with yellow on undersides; often fall prematurely.* CURE: Prevent by ensuring that trees are well supplied with food and water. Gather and burn all infected leaves. Prevent by spraying with ICI General Garden Fungicide. This is only a problem in hot summers.

Shothole *Leaves develop brown spots which eventually fall out to leave small holes.* CURE: See page 73.

Silver Leaf *Leaves on one particular branch (or a few branches) look silvery. When the stem is cut through the wood is found to be stained brown. Shoots may also die back. Purplish bracket fungi may develop on dead branches or trunk.* CURE: See page 73 for this disease and also for **False Silver Leaf.**

For **Aphid** control see page 67.

RASPBERRY

Raspberries require plenty of sun to do well. They will tolerate a wide range of soils providing the drainage is good, but guard against drought in summer.

PROBLEMS

Raspberry Beetle *Fruits eaten by maggots.* CURE: Spray with pbi Liquid Derris, or Murphy Derris Liquid, as soon as the fruits turn pink.

Leaf & Bud Mite *Yellow blotches on upper surface of leaves; no apparent reduction in cropping.* CURE: None. Symptoms resemble those of **Mosaic Virus** but the mites do not significantly reduce either the vigour or the cropping ability of the plants.

Raspberry Mosaic Virus *Leaves distorted and mottled with yellow; few fruits produced.* CURE: Prevent by controlling aphids which spread the disease. Burn infected canes and replant with virus-free stock elsewhere.

Nutrient Deficiency *Leaves yellow between veins; no distortion but slight loss of vigour.* CURE: Very chalky soil causes lime-induced chlorosis. Add plenty of organic matter to prevent this. A lack of manganese or magnesium produces similar symptoms. Fertilise soil well before planting.

Botrytis *Fruits covered with greyish mould.* CURE: Pick off and destroy infected berries. Spray the open flowers in the evening with pbi Benlate and three times more at fortnightly intervals.

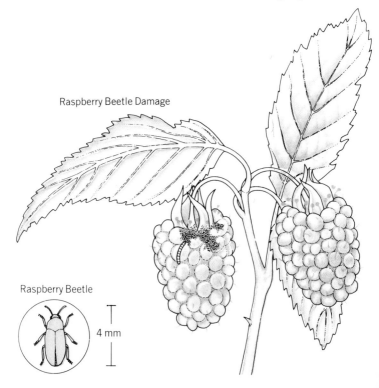

Raspberry Beetle Damage

Raspberry Beetle

4 mm

Cane Blight *Leaves wither, dark marks appear on canes just above soil level; canes become brittle and snap easily.* CURE: Cut out infected canes as far down into the soil as possible. Burn them. Sterilise tools after use. Spray new canes with Synchemicals' Bordeaux Mixture, or Murphy Liquid Copper.

Cane Spot *Small purple spots on canes in early summer turn grey and erupt into small cankers. Spots on leaves and fruits later in season.* CURE: Burn infected canes at end of season. Spray new shoots with pbi Benlate, or Murphy Systemic Fungicide and then at fortnightly intervals until flowers fade.

Spur Blight *Areas of stem around buds turn purplish in late summer, later becoming silver. Infected portion of stem dies. Buds fail to produce shoots in spring, or shoots wilt and die.* CURE: Space canes on framework to allow good air circulation. Burn diseased canes. Spray new shoots with May & Baker Elvaron or pbi Benlate, and give three more sprays at fortnightly intervals.

For **Aphid** control see page 67.

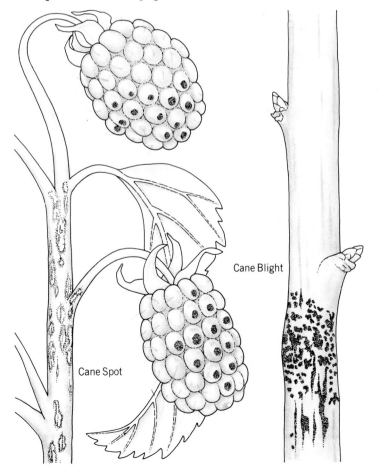

Cane Blight

Cane Spot

STRAWBERRY

Give strawberries a well-drained soil that is not situated in a frost pocket. They will tolerate a little shade and prefer slightly acid ground. Re-make strawberry beds on a fresh site every three years. Always buy healthy 'certified' stock.

PROBLEMS

Eelworm or **Strawberry Mite** *Centre of plant stunted, or leaves marked with reddish brown areas and not fully expanded; leaf stalks may turn red and the flower stems may be extra short.* CURE: None. Burn infected plants. Do not replant on infested ground for at least five years. Always buy certified stock to make sure that the plants are not infested with these pests.

Strawberry Blossom Weevil *Unopened flowers wither and turn brown; flower stalk is partially eaten through.* CURE: Pick off and burn infected flowers.

Red Spider Mite *Leaves pale and bleached; minute mites observed on undersides of leaves; webs spun over foliage in severe attacks.* (See also **Tortrix Moth**.) CURE: Spray at first sign of attack with Bio Systemic Insecticide; Boots Systemic Greenfly Killer, or Murphy Systemic Insecticide. Several sprays will be necessary to give complete control.

Tortrix Moth *Buds, flowers and unopened leaves eaten; leaves wrapped around with silken webs concealing green caterpillars.* CURE: Spray the plants during May with May & Baker Caterpillar Killer, pbi Fenitrothion, or Murphy Fentro.

Strawberry Seed Beetles *The tiny seeds are eaten off fruits as they near maturity, leaving shallow holes which turn brown.* CURE: Prevent by keeping area free of weeds which act as

Strawberry Blossom Weevil Damage   Strawberry Tortrix Moth Damage

alternative hosts. Lay May & Baker Draza Slug pellets, or pbi Slug Gard around plants as a deterrent.

Botrytis *Fruits rotting and covered with grey mould.* CURE: Pick off and destroy any infected fruits. Prevent attack by spraying with pbi Benlate, or Murphy Systemic Fungicide, when the flowers open, and spray three more times at fortnightly intervals.

Strawberry Mildew *Leaves blotched purple on the upper surfaces and covered with white powder on the undersides.* CURE: Spray fortnightly from flower bud formation onwards with pbi Benlate, or Murphy Systemic Fungicide.

Plants become stunted and wilt; eventually die completely. CURE: These symptoms indicate several disorders or diseases which might have to be diagnosed by an expert. Check that the soil is well drained and well supplied with nutrients. Make a new strawberry plantation on fresh ground using certified plants.

Virus Disease *Leaves puckered and distorted; yellow mottling seen; plants stunted; cropping poor.* CURE: None. Burn infected plants. Replant certified stock on new ground. Keep down aphids which spread virus disease.

Frost Damage *Centres of flowers black; petals unaffected.* CURE: Grow plants on a site that is not in a frost pocket. Cover plants with muslin, old net curtains, straw or newspaper if frost threatens at blossom time.

For **Aphid** control see page 67. For **Bird** and **Slug** control see page 52.

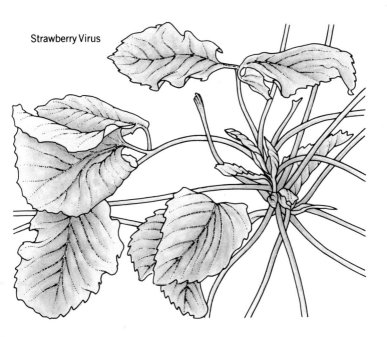

Strawberry Virus

FLOWERS, SHRUBS AND TREES

Unlike vegetables and fruits, flowers are not always grown in large groups of one particular type, and this has the effect of making pest and disease outbreaks less serious. As always there are exceptions, and roses are possibly the most common example. Where such concentrations of one type of plant occur, preventive measures should be adopted, rather than last-ditch attempts at wiping out severe infestations.

Especial care is also needed to prevent accidents in the flower garden, for children and pets are more likely to be at large here than among fruit and vegetables. When you use chemicals in the flower garden, do so in the evening so that bees are harmed as little as possible and the plants have a chance to dry off before small children and animals move among them.

GENERAL PROBLEMS

Honey Fungus or **Armillaria** or **Bootlace Fungus** *Trees, shrubs, and occasionally herbaceous plants, wilt, turn brown and die back for no apparent reason. Parts of hedges may turn brown and die; small, honey-coloured toadstools may appear at the foot of the plant; black bootlace-like growths may be found in the soil, and white fungus seen under the bark at the foot of the plant.* CURE: Burn any badly infected shrubs and plants. Have any dead trees felled and removed (expensive but necessary). Treat infected soil with Bray's Emulsion.

Ants *can be a nuisance in gardens when they infest patios and farm greenfly* **(Aphids)** *on cultivated plants for their honeydew.* CURE: Lay Nippon Ant Destroyer as a poison bait which the ants take back to their nests. This chemical comes in gel form. There are also powder formulations.

For **Aphid, Bird** and **Slug** control see page 52.

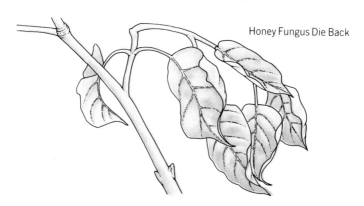

Honey Fungus Die Back

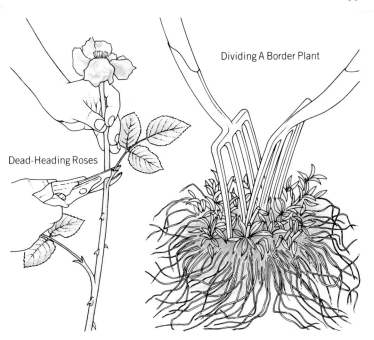

Dividing A Border Plant

Dead-Heading Roses

BORDER PLANTS
There are several operations which should be carried out regularly to keep border plants or 'herbaceous perennials' growing vigorously and therefore resistant to pest and disease attack.

Staking Support flimsy stems by pushing twiggy branches among the plants when they are about 15 cm (6 in) high in spring. The growth will mask the brushwood entirely when it is fully grown. Single stems can be supported either with bamboo canes (tie the plant in loosely with soft twine), or with stout stakes for taller plants such as dahlias and delphiniums. Besides supporting the stems, the stakes also prevent them from rupturing which provides an entry point for disease.

Dead-heading The removal of faded flower heads prevents grey mould (*Botrytis*) from attacking the decaying tissue, and it also encourages the plants to form more flowers rather than seeds. When seed is required, allow the faded blooms to remain on one selected plant.

Thinning Thinning out densely crowded stems helps reduce the risk of fungal diseases which thrive in the centres of overcrowded plants. Reducing the number of stems also encourages the plant to produce better flowers.

Division Old plants should be divided every three years to keep them vigorous and flower productive, otherwise they tend to die out in the middle as they become older.

Feeding Well-fed plants show a marked resistance to pest and disease attack. Give them a dressing of a general fertiliser such as Growmore in spring (two handfuls to 0.83 m^2 (1 sq yd) and monthly foliar feeds in summer.

FLOWERING BULBS

HYACINTH These bulbs are highly valued for their early spring colour and fragrance, both in the house and garden.

PROBLEMS

Black Slime *Leaves turn yellow and collapse and can easily be removed from the bulb which decays. Flat, black resting bodies of the fungus can be found between the outer scales of the bulb.* CURE: Destroy infected bulbs. Do not use the same soil for planting the following year. Always use sterilised compost when growing hyacinths in pots.

Grey Bulb Rot *Top of bulb turns dry and grey either before the leaves appear or shortly after their emergence. Bulb attacked by fungus and black resting bodies found.* CURE: Burn infected bulbs. Do not plant any type of bulb in soil that is near any bed or border where this disease has appeared.

Forcing Fault *Flowers failing to rise up out of leaves.* CURE: Keep potted bulbs outdoors in the cold for at least eight weeks. Bring them indoors and *gradually* introduce them to higher temperatures.

TULIP Short varieties useful for potting; species types for rock garden work and taller varieties for bedding.

PROBLEMS

Tulip Fire *Leaf tips look scorched; strawy marks appear on flowers and rest of leaf.* CURE: Burn infected bulbs. Do not plant in soil known to be infected. Spray emerging leaves with May & Baker Elvaron; pbi Dithane 945, or ICI General Garden Fungicide, and repeat at fortnightly intervals until flowering time.

Virus Disease *Petals distorted and streaked with light or dark lines; leaves may also be streaked and spotted.* CURE: Make sure the colour deviation is not a feature of the tulip variety, e.g. Rembrandt tulips. If not, dig up and burn the plants. Control aphids which spread the virus disease.

Grey Bulb Rot

NARCISSUS
Miniature or tall bulbs suitable for pots, rock gardens, borders or naturalising in grass, provided this is not mown until six weeks after the flowers have faded.

PROBLEMS
Blindness *Leaves produced but no flowers.* CURE: Caused by bulbs being too small. If buds form but turn brown then soil has dried out during flower development, or potted bulbs have been kept in too high a temperature. Plant large bulbs and keep soil moist at all times.

Basal Rot *Base of lifted bulb turns brown and rots in store.* CURE: Destroy all soft or rotting bulbs. Plant firm, healthy bulbs in good soil. Lift and store bulbs in late May.

Bulb Scale Mite *Stored bulbs soft, dry and light; when cut across, brown specks can be seen in the tissue.* CURE: Destroy any bulbs found to be infested with this pest which reduces vigour and causes bulbs to die down prematurely.

Narcissus Fly *No flowers produced; leaves grassy and lacking in vigour. Large caterpillar found if bulb cut open.* CURE: Destroy infested bulbs. Buy bulbs from a reputable supplier who has treated them against this pest. Where pest occurs in naturalised plantings, dust leaves and soil fortnightly after flowering until June with Murphy Gamma-BHC Dust.

Smoulder *Stored bulbs rot; black resting bodies found on outside of bulb. In wet springs leaves and flowers may show signs of rot and some spotting.* CURE: Destroy stored bulbs that are infected. Spray leaves with pbi Benlate at first sign of attack.

Stem & Bulb Eelworm *Leaves distorted and mottled with yellow; flowers also distorted or absent altogether. When sliced open laterally, bulb shows brown rings.* CURE: Buy bulbs from a reputable supplier. Destroy any that are found to be infested with this pest and do not plant any bulbs in ground known to be infested.

Stem and Bulb Eelworm Damage

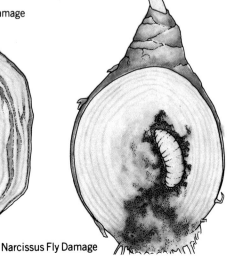

Narcissus Fly Damage

ANNUALS AND BEDDING PLANTS

Most annuals and bedding plants grow so quickly in good compost that they do not have time to be struck down by pests and diseases, but there are always exceptions, and the common blights may strike anywhere.

GENERAL PROBLEMS
Caterpillars *Leaves eaten; no slime trails seen.* CURE: Pick off caterpillars and destroy if outbreak is small. Spray larger infestations with ICI Sybol 2, pbi Fenitrothion, or Murphy Fentro.
Botrytis *Parts of plant rotting and covered with grey/brown mould.* CURE: Cut off and destroy infected parts. Spray with pbi Benlate.

SPECIFIC PROBLEMS
Antirrhinum Rust *Antirrhinums (snapdragons) develop dark brown spots on leaves and stems.* CURE: Pull up and burn badly infected plants. Grow rust-resistant varieties. Spray fortnightly with pbi Dithane 945.
Mosaic Virus *Sweet pea leaves become mottled and the stems streaked; the plant wilts.* CURE: None. Destroy infected plants and wash tools and hands to avoid spreading the disease. Control aphids which spread virus disease.
Blackleg or **Foot Rot** *Plants rot off at soil level.* CURE: Raise plants in sterile compost. Avoid waterlogging. Water seedlings with Cheshunt Compound to prevent attack. Pull up any affected plants.
Clubroot *Wallflowers wilt and when pulled up roots are found to be swollen.* CURE: Avoid growing in land known to be infected or where brassicas have previously been grown. Lime very acid soils. Dip young plants in Murphy Systemic Clubroot Dip before planting.

For **Aphid** and **Slug** control see page 52.

Rhododendron Bud Blast

RHODODENDRON Large evergreen or deciduous
flowering shrubs; the smaller types are often known as azaleas.

PROBLEMS
Azalea Gall *Green or red swellings appear on leaves and
eventually turn white. They shrivel and turn brown later.* CURE:
Remove and burn galls as soon as they are seen. Spray plant
with Synchemicals' Bordeaux Mixture, or Murphy Liquid
Copper Fungicide, and repeat each spring.

Bud Blast *Buds turn brown and refuse to open; little black
pinhead-like outgrowths appear all over them.* CURE: Cut off
and burn all infected buds. Spray plants with Murphy Fentro,
or pbi Fenitrothion, in late summer and early autumn to
control leaf hoppers which allow disease to enter.

Vine Weevil *Lower leaves are eaten and left looking tattered.*
CURE: If damage is severe dust lower leaves and soil with
Murphy Gamma-BHC Dust.

Chlorosis *Leaves yellow between veins.* CURE: Prevent by
growing rhododendrons on lime-free soil. Incorporate plenty
of organic matter. Where soil is only just acid, water on diluted
Iron Sequestrene once a month during spring and summer.

Rhododendron Bug *Leaves mottled with yellow on the upper
surface; russeted below; small lacy-winged insects may be
observed.* CURE: Spray undersides of leaves with ICI Sybol 2,
pbi Fenitrothion, or Murphy Fentro.

ROSE (Rosa) Favourite garden shrubs which usually grow and flower well in spite of being subject to a number of diseases and beloved of a handful of pests.

PROBLEMS

Capsid Bug *Young leaves punctured and distorted by this fast-moving green insect; punctures develop brown edges as leaf ages.* CURE: Spray with Bio Systemic Insecticide, Boots Systemic Greenfly Killer, or Murphy Systemic Insecticide as the leaves unfurl in spring and summer.

Caterpillars *Leaves eaten and caterpillars found among them.* CURE: Hand pick in isolated outbreaks. Spray larger infestations with May & Baker Caterpillar Killer or ICI Sybol 2.

Cuckoo Spit *Blobs of white froth at stem tips; insects inside sucking sap.* CURE: Rub off by hand in small outbreaks. Larger infestations can be controlled by spraying forcefully with Murphy Fentro, or pbi Fenitrothion.

Leafcutter Bee *Leaves broadly scalloped and pieces completely removed.* CURE: None.

Leaf-Rolling Sawfly *Leaves rolled under longitudinally; green caterpillars may be present inside.* CURE: Pick off isolated leaves that are curled. If the pest has previously been a problem, spray the plants with May & Baker Caterpillar Killer, or ICI Sybol 2 in late May and again in mid-June.

Rose Blackspot *Blackish purple spots 6 mm (¼ in) diameter appear on lower leaves first – later higher up the plant. They join together, the leaf turns yellow and falls prematurely.* CURE:

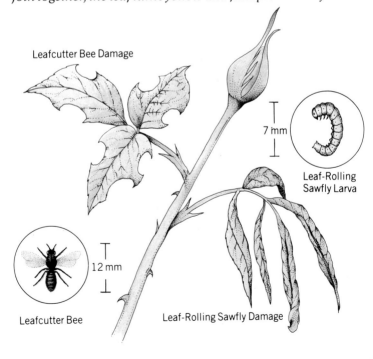

Leafcutter Bee Damage

7 mm

Leaf-Rolling Sawfly Larva

12 mm

Leafcutter Bee

Leaf-Rolling Sawfly Damage

Prevent by burning all fallen leaves at the end of the season, and by picking off infected leaves. Spray fortnightly with ICI Nimrod-T from early May onwards. Spray soil as well.

Canker *Rough, sunken, brown areas appear on the stem which will die if it is encircled.* CURE: Cut out all infected stems cleanly into healthy wood. Paint the cut surfaces with May & Baker Seal & Heal Pruning Paint. Spray at the same time with Murphy Liquid Copper Fungicide, or Synchemicals' Bordeaux Mixture. In future prune carefully and feed plants well.

Rose Mildew *Leaves, stems and thorns covered with white powder and severely weakened.* CURE: Prune to produce an open, well-ventilated bush where fungus diseases will be less prevalent. Pick off and burn badly infected leaves, and start preventive fortnightly sprays in early May using ICI Nimrod-T (which will also control **Blackspot**). Grow resistant varieties. Prune out badly infected shoots in autumn.

Rose Rust *Small orange spots appear on undersides of leaves and later orange streaks appear on stems and leaf stalks. Leaves eventually wither and fall.* CURE: Cut out any shoots or leaves that show signs of attack. Keep bushes growing healthily and spray with pbi Dithane at fortnightly intervals.

Rose Sickness *New bushes planted in old rose beds appear weak and may die back.* CURE: Do not plant new bushes on ground occupied for many years by roses. If unavoidable, dig out and replace the soil to a depth of 60 cm (2 ft).

For **Aphid** control see page 52.

Blackspot

Mildew

LAWNS

Most lawns are subjected to continuous hard wear, yet far too few gardeners lavish any care on their grass; it is simply shorn off every week through the spring and summer, and maybe given one feed at the start of the season. To grow a good, hard-wearing lawn the following tasks are well worth carrying out.

Mowing Never mow when the grass is wet or frosted. Except in very hot weather, always remove the clippings if you want to achieve a fine lawn (this means raking them up if your mower does not possess a grass box or bag). Do not cut ordinary lawns too low – 2 cm (¾ in) is usually sufficient and will produce a hard-wearing surface. Start to mow in spring as soon as the grass begins to grow, and continue into autumn when the weather allows. The grass should not be cut too low at the beginning or end of the season. Mow the lawn in a different direction each time.

Aerating In spring, go over your lawn with a garden fork or special turf aerator. Stab it into the surface every 15 cm (6 in) or so to a depth of 7 cm (3 in). This will improve surface drainage and relieve compaction.

Scarifying After aerating, vigorously comb the lawn with a wire-toothed rake to pull out dead grass and moss. This action can be repeated in autumn.

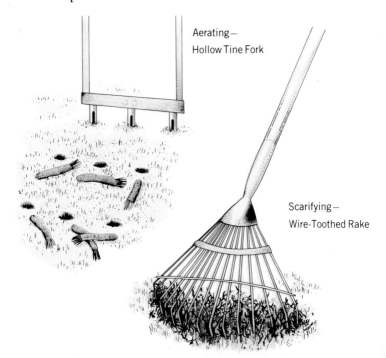

Aerating —
Hollow Tine Fork

Scarifying —
Wire-Toothed Rake

Feeding Scatter a proprietary lawn fertiliser (or a fertiliser and weedkiller combined) on the lawn in April and water it in if no rain is forthcoming within the next day or two. Two further applications of lawn food can be made through the summer, but if you feed in autumn, use a product which is recommended for application at that time of year. Fertilisers high in nitrogen will encourage sappy, frost-tender growth if applied after August.

Watering Right through the summer the lawn should be given a really good soak if it starts to get dry. Invest in a lawn sprinkler and leave this running for an hour or so in any one spot so that the soil is well moistened.

Algae

LAWN PROBLEMS

Algae *Dark green slimy areas on the lawn are usually caused by algae. They thrive in damp soil which is badly drained or shaded by trees and shrubs.* CURE: Spike and aerate the lawn to help surface drainage, and treat the areas with Bio Moss Killer, Murphy Super Moss Killer and Lawn Fungicide, or May & Baker Mosstox-Plus.

Ants *Ants can make a nuisance of themselves on lawns where picnics are popular. They are common on paved areas where their nests are made beneath the stones. On lawns they will bring up piles of fine soil which are then flattened by the mower – creating a site for weed growth.* CURE: Dust nests with Synchemicals' Nippon Ant Powder.

Birds *Many birds are beneficial on lawns – starlings will make a significant contribution to the removal of leatherjackets and earthworms – but when a new lawn has been sown the seed eaters can be a nuisance.* CURE: Scatter more seed than is necessary on the ground where the lawn is being made. This will allow the birds to feast without reducing the required density of the grass. Buy seed treated with a bird repellent (which will eventually wash off). Lay twiggy branches over the area to prevent sparrows from enjoying dust baths and disturbing the surface of the soil.

Damping Off *Newly germinated grass seedlings may wilt and die – the bases of the blades becoming yellow or brown and rotten. This is especially common in very humid or wet weather.* CURE: Ensure that the site is well drained before sowing. At the first sign of the disease, water the affected areas with Cheshunt Compound diluted at the rate of 14 g (½ oz) in 4.54 litres (1 gall) of water. Apply 4.54 litres (1 gall) to 0.83 m² (1 sq yd).

Dogs *Bitch urine can cause burning of the turf. The affected area will become straw coloured and may be surrounded by a circle of dark green grass.* CURE: Spike the area with a fork and drench it with water as soon as the dog is seen to have fouled the area. The same treatment can be adopted when the grass appears strawy but recovery will be slow.

Dollar Spot *Small straw-coloured patches 2.5-5 cm (1-2 in) across may appear on the lawn in August and September during humid weather. They will slowly enlarge and join together.* CURE: Water affected areas with a solution of sulphate of iron diluted in water at the rate of 28 g (1 oz) in 9 litres (2 gall). Apply 2.2 litres (½ gall) of the solution to 0.83 m² (1 sq yd) of affected turf. Prevent the disease from attacking by making sure that the lawn is well fed.

Fairy Rings *Large rings or part rings of dark green grass spread outwards and become larger. On close examination it may be seen that a ring of weak or dead grass is sandwiched between two rings of dark green grass. Toadstools may appear in the outer green ring in summer or autumn.* CURE: Water infected turf with sulphate of iron diluted in water at the rate of 448 g (1 lb) in 6.8 litres (1½ gall). Apply 2.2 litres (½ gall) of the solution to 0.83 m² (1 sq yd). Severe infestations can only be controlled by cutting away the affected turf (remove 30 cm (1 ft) of seemingly unaffected grass at either side of the ring as well). The soil should then be forked over and watered with a 2 per cent formalin solution. Leave the soil covered with polythene for a week before incorporating new soil and re-sowing.

Fusarium Patch (Snow Mould) *The grass turns yellow in patches before going brown and dying. Pinkish white fungal strands may be noticed among the grass. This fungus disease is most common in humid weather and often occurs on lawns which are not well drained or on grass which has been too closely mown rather than on coarser turf. It may also occur if the lawn has been walked on while covered in snow.* CURE: Dilute sulphate of iron in water at the rate of 28 g (1 oz) to 9 litres (2 gall) and apply 2.2 litres (½ gall) to 0.83 m² (1 sq yd). Prevent attack by undertaking spiking and scarification as advised on page 92, and do not apply high nitrogen fertilisers such as sulphate of ammonia after August.

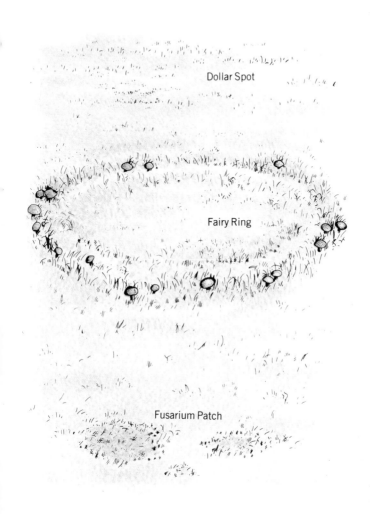

Dollar Spot

Fairy Ring

Fusarium Patch

Leatherjackets *Patches of grass turn yellow but there is no sign of fungal growth. Soak a patch of soil in the evening and cover it with a polythene sheet or sack. Grey grubs (larvae of the daddy-longlegs) will be found on the surface in the morning if leatherjackets are responsible.* CURE: Dust the turf with Murphy Gamma-BHC Dust in September or October, or spray at the same time with Murphy Lindex Garden Spray.

INDEX